The Art and Power
of Facilitation

Running Powerful
Meetings

The Art and Power
of Facilitation

Running Powerful
Meetings

Alice Zavala, PMP
Kathleen B. Hass, PMP

MANAGEMENTCONCEPTS

𝄢
MANAGEMENTCONCEPTS
8230 Leesburg Pike, Suite 800
Vienna, VA 22182
703.790.9595
Fax: 703.790.1371
www.managementconcepts.com

Printed in the United States of America

Library of Congress Cataloging-in-Publication Data

Zavala, Alice.
  The art and power of facilitation: running powerful meetings / Alice Zavala and Kathleen B. Hass.
    p. cm. -- (Business analysis essentials library)
  ISBN-13: 978-1-56726-212-4
  1. Group facilitation. 2. Business meetings. I. Hass, Kathleen B. II. Title.

HM751.Z38 2008
658.4'56--dc22   2007027820

10   9   8   7   6   5   4   3   2   1

About the Authors

Alice Zavala is a senior management professional with over 25 years of experience in program and project management, operational management, sales and marketing, information technology, customer service, training, curriculum design, and formal facilitation. Her experience spans numerous industries and organizations, including the SABRE Group, Delta Air Lines, American Air Lines, Toyota Financial Services, CitiFinancial Auto, Constellation Energy, and multiple federal agencies including NARA, OPM, and an agency within the intelligence community.

Ms. Zavala specializes in designing, launching, and improving project management offices, project management maturity assessments, requirements maturity management, developing and implementing coaching and mentoring programs, designing and implementing enterprise portfolio management methods, planning and executing projects, rescuing troubled projects, and business process reengineering.

Kathleen B. Hass is the Project Management and Business Analysis Practice Leader for Management Concepts. Ms. Hass is a prominent presenter at industry conferences and is an author and lecturer in strategic project management and business analysis disciplines. Her expertise includes leading technology and software-intensive projects, building and leading strategic project teams, and conducting program management for large, complex engagements. Ms. Hass has more than 25 years of experience in project management and business analysis, including project portfolio management implementation, project office creation and management, business process reengineering, IT applications development and technology deployment, project management and business analysis training and mentoring, and requirements management. Ms. Hass has managed large, complex projects in the airline, telecommunications, retail, and manufacturing industries and in the U.S. federal government.

Ms. Hass' consulting experience includes engagements with multiple agencies within the federal government, such as USDA, USGS, NARA, and an agency within the intelligence community, as well as industry engagements at Colorado Springs Utilities, Toyota Financial Services, Toyota Motor Sales, the Salt Lake Organizing Committee for the 2002 Olympic Winter Games, Hilti US Inc., The SABRE Group, Sulzer Medica, and Qwest Communications. Client services have included maturity assessment, project quality and risk assessment, project launches, troubled project recovery, risk management, and implementation of program management offices and strategic planning and project portfolio management processes.

Ms. Hass earned a B.A. in business administration with summa cum laude honors from Western Connecticut University.

Table of Contents

Preface

The Business Analysis Essential Library is a series of books that each cover a separate and distinct area of business analysis. The business analyst is the project member who ensures that there is a strong business focus for the projects that emerge as a result of the fierce, competitive nature and rapid rate of change of business today. Within both private industry and government agencies, the business analyst is becoming the central figure in leading major change initiatives. This library is designed to explain the emerging role of the business analyst and present contemporary business analysis practices (the what), supported by practical tools and techniques to enable the application of the practices (the how). Current books in the series are:

- *Professionalizing Business Analysis: Breaking the Cycle of Challenged Projects*

- *The Business Analyst as Strategist: Translating Business Strategies into Valuable Solutions*

- *Unearthing Business Requirements: Elicitation Tools and Techniques*

- *Getting it Right: Business Requirement Analysis Tools and Techniques*

- *The Art and Power of Facilitation: Running Powerful Meetings*

- *From Analyst to Leader: Elevating the Role of the Business Analyst*

Check the Management Concepts website, www.managementconcepts.com/pubs, for updates to this series.

About This Book

The goal of this book is to arm the business analyst with principles, practices, and tools for effective facilitation and meeting management, with a focus on meetings the business analyst is likely to lead. The business analyst's role is all about the art of driving various constituencies through processes to achieve consensus on the needs of the business. A business analyst who is an expert facilitator does this in a manner that encourages participation and ownership and that maximizes the productivity of everyone involved in requirements definition and management.

Some business analysis activities take place in one-on-one interviews. Conducting a good interview is a valuable business analysis skill, and we will provide some useful insights on how to plan and conduct an effective interview. However, most business analysis work to elicit, analyze, specify, and validate requirements is done in some type of meeting. The goal of this book is to equip the business analyst with several powerful tools to successfully negotiate through the myriad meetings, informal working sessions, and formal workshops that are necessary to develop business requirements.

Chapter 1

To Meet or Not to Meet, That Is the Question

In This Chapter:

- Think Before You Meet

- Meeting Types

The business analyst uses different types of meetings—one-on-one interviews, small-group working sessions, or formal requirements elicitation workshops—and various facilitation techniques to get the job done. The ability to plan and facilitate effective meetings, bring a group to consensus, and drive resolution of issues and conflicts is essential to the successful business analyst. Therefore, meeting planning and facilitation is at the core of the business analyst's skill set. As Ellen Gottesdiener notes in *Requirements by Collaboration*:[1]

> The cost of ineffective meetings is staggering. The average person attends seven to ten meetings a week, half of which are unproductive, and the average meeting involves nine people...who have as little as two hours' prior notice.

People come together in teams to complete project work, and yet the underlying group meeting process is often poorly managed. The successful business analyst becomes adept at planning and facilitating sessions for groups of people, conscious and respectful of the participants' time. As facilitator, the business analyst is ever mindful that when people work in teams, there are two equally challenging dynamics at play. Being results-oriented by nature, people focus on the *purpose* of the meeting, so that work is actually accomplished. Frequently this is the only issue team members consider. The second dimension of meetings is the *process* of the group work itself—the mechanisms by which the group acts as a team and not simply as people who happen to be together in a room.

If due attention is not paid to the meeting process, the value of bringing people together can be diminished. Expert management of the meeting process can enhance the value of the group to many times the sum of the worth of the individuals. It is this synergy that makes project work rewarding. The astute business analyst examines the group process and discovers how to quickly transition a group of people that have come together in a meeting into a highly effective team. The goal is for the group of people at the business analysis meeting to be viewed as an important resource whose time and effort must be managed just like any other corporate asset.[2]

Think Before You Meet

Meeting facilitation and management skills are often overlooked by both project managers and business analysts, the critical project team members who lead multiple kinds of meetings. Because it is clear that meetings are very expensive activities when the cost of labor for the meeting participants and the opportunity cost of spending time on a more effective activity are considered, the professional business analyst takes meeting facilitation and management very seriously.

The first thing to determine is whether a meeting is truly required. For the business analyst, the answer to this question is often a resounding "yes," but let us explore the question a little further. According to Miranda Duncan[3], there are several reasons to hold a meeting, which are shown in Table 1-1.

Table 1-1—Purposes and Goals at Meetings

Meeting Purpose	Goal
Information exchange	Acquiring or disseminating information, or both
Self-awareness or consciousness-raising	Building support
Learning	Imparting knowledge and skills
Creative thinking	Generating ideas, innovation
Critical thinking	Analysis, goal setting, problem-solving, decision-making
Accomplishing tasks	Creating work products, e.g., requirements statements and models
Team building	Building relationships and commitment

Clearly, the business analyst needs to accomplish all the goals in Table 1-1 from time to time. However, it is not always necessary to hold a meeting to accomplish a goal. Sometimes alternatives to holding a meeting just might work as well or even better. Consider the alternatives shown in Table 1-2.

Table 1-2—Alternatives to Meetings

Meeting Purpose	Non-Meeting Alternatives
To generate ideas	Surveys, worksheets, anonymous brainstorming
To share information	Conference calls, emails, communiqués
To solve a problem or make a decision	Surveys, multivoting by secret ballot

Contemplate the following questions to determine whether a meeting is needed:

+ Is sufficient information available at the time of the meeting to present, consider, and decide on a course of action?

+ Is the objective of the meeting clearly defined? Is there a specific result to be achieved? Are there actions to be taken?

+ Is there a less costly way to achieve the same result?

‣ Is it clear who must attend to attain the meeting's objectives? Are they able to attend—or to be represented by someone authorized to make decisions on behalf of their group?

‣ Are there compelling secondary advantages to holding a meeting (e.g., team building, problem solving, brainstorming, information sharing)?

Meeting Types

Once it is clear that a meeting is needed to accomplish your objectives, consider the type of meeting that will best suit the situation. Types of meetings are shown in Table 1-3.

Table 1-3—Meeting Types

Meeting Type	Meeting Description	Examples
Informational meeting	An arranged gathering of two or more participants to share information	‣ Project status meeting ‣ Staff meeting
Workshop	A facilitated set of activities designed to guide and promote participation of selected stakeholders to work toward a defined outcome or results	‣ Requirements elicitation workshop to document business needs ‣ Kickoff meeting to launch a new project
Interview	A one-on-one meeting for the purpose of obtaining information, identifying issues, and building consensus on key concepts	‣ Interview with members of management to determine their expectations of the new business solution
Focus group	A facilitated group interview of persons with a common demographic for the purpose of obtaining information, identifying issues, and building consensus on key concepts	‣ Meeting with customer groups to define the business problem or opportunity ‣ Meeting with similar types of end users to determine how they will use the new product
Working session	An arranged gathering of two or more participants to analyze a business process, develop requirements understanding models, generate ideas, solve a problem, or make a decision	‣ Core team session to conduct a feasibility study and build a business case for a proposed new project ‣ Modeling meeting to document a business process ‣ Quality review meeting to validate requirements

The business analyst typically uses all the meeting types listed in Table 1-3. Workshops, focus groups, and informal working sessions are most effective when conducted by a business analyst who is also a skilled facilitator—one who brings meeting design, process, tools, techniques, and expertise to produce the desired outcome. The greatest challenge for the business analyst is to effectively facilitate the various types of meetings throughout the project. The ultimate goals are to:

+ Identify and document the true business need

+ Foster a collaborative environment for identifying, analyzing, verifying, and validating the requirements

+ Enable stakeholders with differing needs and priorities to make decisions, work out conflicts, and resolve issues

+ Foster creativity and innovation to produce the best solution to meet the business need

+ Encourage the various stakeholders to make decisions based on value that will be created for the business versus individual groups' needs and wants

Why is facilitating effective meetings so challenging? Table 1-4 lists just a few of the meeting inadequacies and adverse results that we will address in the remaining chapters of this book.

Table 1-4—Meeting Inadequacies and Results

Meeting Inadequacies	Result
The meeting purpose is unclear because of inadequate planning or facilitation	• Meetings are ineffective, objectives are not achieved, and ultimately the credibility of the business analyst is questioned
The meeting agenda and facilitation techniques are not designed to achieve the intended outcome	• Agendas do not support the meeting purpose • Participants arrive unprepared • Key participants do not attend • Inappropriate discussions ensue
Too many meetings are needed to accomplish the objectives	• Increasing the time and cost of the effort to elicit and validate requirements results in loss of confidence in the requirements process
The meeting results are not transcribed and provided to the participants for their review and refinement in a timely manner	• The perception is that little value was provided by the outcome of the meeting
Meetings are too long	• Energy is drained from the group • Participants are physically and mentally fatigued • Quality of outcomes is reduced • Meetings are perceived to be too costly

In the following chapters we explore general meeting planning and management techniques and facilitation practices designed to avoid the pitfalls that lead to unproductive meetings. Read Chapter 2 to gain an understanding of the basics of planning, facilitating, and managing effective meetings. Refer to Chapter 2 whenever you are planning meeting agenda items and thinking about facilitation techniques to ensure that you do not skip any critical preparation steps. Chapters 3 and 4 provide you with an understanding of the art and power of facilitation and hopefully will motivate you to seek out other books, classes, and new experiences so that you can become an expert facilitator.

The remaining chapters provide information about meetings that are planned, organized, facilitated, and managed by the business analyst.

Endnotes

1. Ellen Gottesdiener. *Requirements by Collaboration: Workshops for Defining Needs*, 2002. Boston: Addison-Wesley.

2. Gerard M. Blair. *Groups That Work.* Online at www.see.ed.ac.uk/~gerard/Management/art0.html (accessed August 9, 2007).

3. Miranda Duncan. *Effective Meeting Facilitation: Sample Forms, Tools, and Checklists*, 1996. Available online through the National Endowment for the Arts' Lessons Learned Toolsite, www.nea.gov/resources/Lessons/Duncan2.html (accessed on August 16, 2007).

Chapter 2

Meeting Management Best Practices

In This Chapter:

- Establish the Meeting Foundation
- Design the Meeting to Meet the Objectives
- Determine the Meeting Participants
- Prepare the Meeting Agenda
- Open the Meeting
- Establish Meeting Ground Rules
- Conduct the Meeting Using Appropriate Facilitation Techniques
- Close the Meeting
- Followup after the Meeting

Meeting management skills are often undervalued and underrated in the business environment, even though meetings consume so much valuable time and so many critical resources. Why is so little effort expended to make meetings more effective? Here are a few reasons to consider:

+ Business leaders do not recognize the relationship between ineffective meetings and the productivity measures of their organization.

+ Mid-level managers do not have the knowledge or the skills needed to plan, conduct, and facilitate an effective meeting and then follow up on decisions.

+ Project managers and business analysts do not appreciate the importance of planning a meeting for better results.

+ The cost drain from ineffective meetings is not recognized.

+ Management does not hold functional managers, business analysts, project managers, or other persons accountable for the impacts of ineffective meetings.

Although the business analyst facilitates multiple types of meetings, following some basic steps results in effective and efficient use of participants' time and a positive outcome for everyone. Note: Although these steps appear to be conducted sequentially, in practice they are likely to be completed iteratively:

1. Establish the meeting foundation.

2. Design the meeting to meet the objectives.

3. Determine the meeting participants.

4. Prepare the meeting agenda.

5. Open the meeting.

6. Establish meeting ground rules.

7. Conduct the meeting using appropriate facilitation techniques.

8. Close the meeting.

9. Follow up after the meeting.

Each step is explained briefly in the sections that follow.

Establish the Meeting Foundation

Before you jump into planning the meeting, determine the objectives and purpose of the meeting by answering the following questions:

+ Describe the purpose or goal of the meeting—*Why* have you decided to have a meeting?

+ Define the meeting objectives—*How* will the goal be achieved?

+ Describe the desired outcome of the meeting—*What* product or deliverable will be produced or decision made that constitutes meeting success?

+ Determine how to measure the effectiveness of the meeting—*How* will you measure the success of the meeting?

+ Clearly understand who needs the meeting deliverables—*Who* will use the output?

+ Determine the use of the meeting deliverables—*How* will the output be used to add value to the project?

Design the Meeting to Meet the Objectives

Once the meeting's purpose, objectives, and outcomes are well understood, the business analyst determines the most appropriate meeting type from among the alternatives presented in the preceding chapter. Do not hold a formal meeting with a large number of participants when a small, informal working session will accomplish the meeting objectives. Keep in mind the cost of large meetings, the difficulty in reaching consensus when the group is large, and the value of small-group interactions. All the people invited to the meeting will expect ample time to air their viewpoints and participate fully in the discussion and the decisions.

The business analyst designs the meeting on the basis of the objectives and purpose of the session. Preparations for an informal working session are likely to be less rigorous than preparations for a formal requirements elicitation workshop. But no matter how small or informal the meeting, success is directly related to adequate meeting preparation.

Determine the Meeting Participants

Identify the appropriate participants to be invited to the meeting. Ensure that they have been authorized to dedicate time to your effort and that they are empowered not only to represent their organization but also to make decisions and commitments on behalf of it. When selecting meeting participants, consider the experience level, knowledge and skills, and availability of the persons you need to accomplish the meeting objectives.

Ensure that all stakeholders who will be affected by the outcome of the meeting are represented, including members of management, business unit representatives, technical experts, and virtual team members. It is almost always necessary for the business analyst to include technical representatives and the project manager in requirements sessions in which key decisions are to be made. Collaborating with others when building the meeting attendee list is a good practice. As a courtesy, try to speak with participants before they receive your meeting invitation so that they will not be surprised. This small gesture goes a long way in building trust among the team members.

If the meeting requires large participation, it is likely that the meeting must be scheduled far in advance so that key attendees can block out the time in their calendars. Considerations include company, organization, and department calendars, as well as individual commitments and meeting room availability. The organization's meeting culture must also be considered. The business analyst should take into account cultural considerations like:

+ **Meeting tolerance.** Don't expect participants to be taken away from their business unit for meetings too often, such as more than two or three days in a week.

+ **Political agendas.** Conduct several meeting preparation interviews with key members of management and others who are influential within the organization to avoid political hazards. Political mistakes can be devastating to the effort to build a collaborative environment.

+ **Meeting history.** There might be some unwritten rules about meetings. Again, conduct premeeting interviews to learn the meeting norms.

+ **Team collaboration.** Take into account the amount of collaboration and team spirit that you have been able to engender to this point. Schedule less important meetings when the group is just coming together and critical meetings after you have had a chance to work with the group and gain its trust.

+ **Management structure.** Be sure to respect the chain of command when considering the attendees. In addition, make sure you have management approval to use their resources to capture, document, and validate requirements.

Prepare the Meeting Agenda

An agenda is a structured set of activities designed to produce the work products that will achieve the meeting objectives. There are two types of agendas:

+ **Meeting agenda.** An agenda used by meeting participants that includes the meeting topics, activities, presenters, and timelines.

+ **Facilitator agenda.** An extension of the meeting agenda that includes the facilitation approach, tools, and techniques used for each meeting topic to ensure that meeting objectives are met.

Knowing the purpose of the meeting is the first step in structuring the agenda. Having a firm idea of where you want to be by the end of the meeting suggests what must be covered during the meeting. The business analyst uses a very different set of agenda items to develop requirement functions or features than he uses to prioritize predefined requirements. Each step in reaching the desired meeting outcome is thought through carefully to determine the specific activity, how it will be facilitated, and the amount of time needed. Steps include:

+ Establish how long the meeting is to last; shorter is better than longer.

+ List the agenda items that need to be covered or process steps that need to occur.

+ Determine the facilitation technique to be used for each agenda item.

+ Build in time for key experts to be heard.

+ Estimate how long each item will take, factoring in time for dialogue.

+ Leave a minimum of 15 minutes at the end for summary and agreement on what comes next.

If, after completing these steps, the agenda clearly requires more time, revise it accordingly. You might need to adjust the length of the meeting or cut back on what you expect to accomplish. Keep in mind that critical thinking requires more time than what is typically allowed, especially if there is controversy. In addition, as the number of meeting participants increases, you need more generous time allotments so that everyone can participate. Opportunities to voice an opinion, ask questions, and explain reasons behind positions are critical to developing and achieving consensus. Shortcuts at this point could cause looping back or gridlock.

To build a collaborative environment even before the meeting, enlist key participants to assist in developing the agenda, especially the project manager, technical lead, lead business representative, and key subject matter experts. Clearly state the overall outcome to be achieved at the end of the meeting and any preparation the participants are expected to complete before the meeting. Carter McNamara, MBA, Ph.D., of Authenticity Consulting, LLC, offers these tips for designing effective agendas:[1]

+ *Include something in the agenda for participants to do right away so they come on time and get involved early.*

- *Next to each major topic, include the type of action needed, the type of output expected (decision, vote, action assigned to someone), and time estimates for addressing each topic.*

- *Don't overdesign meetings; be willing to change the meeting agenda if members are making progress with certain agenda items.*

- *Think about how you label an event so people come in with that global-use mind set. It might pay to have a short dialogue around the meeting title to develop a common mind set among attendees, particularly if they include representatives from various cultures.*

Because the business analyst designs each meeting to produce an output or a deliverable, the stakes are high. Planning an effective requirements elicitation, analysis, specification, or validation meeting requires the business analyst to prepare extensively for each event to accomplish the following:

- Determine the appropriate requirements artifacts to be produced as a result of the meeting, including the method, tools, and templates that will be used. (An *artifact* is a requirement work product, such as a document, table, matrix, or diagram.)

- Select the appropriate decision process to be used to arrive at consensus on the meeting results.

- Design the appropriate facilitation activities and techniques for use to guide the participants to discover, create, and verify requirements.

- Determine how to facilitate the interaction among meeting participants; for example, will the participants break out into small groups or work as a whole?

+ Determine the appropriate visual media to facilitate understanding and consensus, such as flip charts, posters, sticky notes, cards on the wall, diagrams, and other visual aids.

+ Ensure that the participants have prepared for the meeting, including possibly creating straw man work products to be used as a starting point to create requirements deliverables.

Although many books on meeting planning are available, there are a few special considerations for the business analyst. While making room reservations and sending out invitations, the business analyst is also finalizing the facilitator agenda that contains the tools, templates, visuals, supplies, and facilitation techniques to be used to facilitate each agenda item. If the outcome of the meeting is complex, the business analyst almost always works with small groups to create a draft version of the deliverables before the meeting and then facilitates the review and refinement of the deliverable during the meeting with the larger group. In addition, the business analyst confirms that the appropriate business and technical representatives will be available to attend the meeting and follow-up sessions. If not, the meeting should be rescheduled. For significant meetings, the business analyst invites the participants under the signature of the project or business sponsor. Attachments to the workshop invitation include a finalized agenda and summary-level project documents, which the participants should review before the meeting.

The setup of the room is important to the success of a requirements elicitation meeting. Arrange the room for optimal efficiency and comfort during the session. For a requirements elicitation workshop, a U-shape setup (Figure 2-1) is the best possible setup to ensure effective communication and participation of all workshop attendees.

Figure 2-1—Room Setup

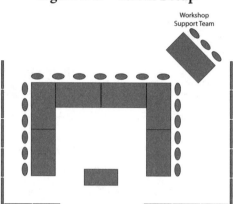

Table 2-1 has tips for organizing a formal workshop.

Table 2-1—Tips for Organizing a Formal Workshop

Setup Item	Description
Seating arrangement	The participants should be seated around tables arranged in a U shape or in pods of teams.
Handouts	A packet of information, in the form of requirements drafted to date and other key project information, should be placed at each participant's seat. In addition to the draft requirements, this packet may contain the agenda, the list of participants, a copy of the mission/business case, the project charter, the project management plan, the requirements management plan, the issues log, the risk log, the milestone schedule, and any other prepared information that is pertinent to the meeting.
Supplies	In addition to the project information, note pads, name tents, pens, ice water, and glasses should be readily available for the participants. The facilitators will need flip charts and paper, poster paper, "sticky notes," markers, note pads, pens, an LCD/PC viewer/projector, a printer, etc. A checklist of supplies and equipment is helpful.
Meeting planning team	A table should be set to the side or back of the room for the meeting facilitator/scribe team. They will need supplies such as laptop computers, a printer, and disks for capturing and printing all the information gathered during the workshop. The team will capture information in real time to present to the participants periodically for their review and refinement.

Open the Meeting

As participants arrive for the meeting, greet them by name and make introductions. Set the precedent by starting the meeting on time, even if some participants have not arrived. Introduce yourself and describe your role as the business analyst and meeting facilitator. Also introduce other key members who helped to prepare for the meeting, as well as those who will help conduct the meeting and capture the information. Review the agenda and discuss the goals of the meeting to get everyone prepared for the work ahead. Ask if the agenda as structured will meet everyone's expectations. If not, ask if there are any recommended adjustments to the agenda. Be prepared to incorporate the recommendations if they would help to achieve the meeting objectives. This approach secures everyone's agreement to the agenda. You might even ask that everyone help manage the group's time by keeping to the agenda. Review the project objectives, relate the meeting to the project objectives, and briefly discuss expected follow-on activities. Then ask the members to introduce themselves. If it is the first meeting of the group, plan a warm-up activity that helps the team members get to know each other.

Before plunging into the agenda, define roles and responsibilities and discuss how the group will work together in the future. Emphasize the need for everyone to participate, contribute to understanding issues and problems, and help drive the group to consensus decisions.

Establish Meeting Ground Rules

Setting ground rules before the meeting work begins is helpful, especially for working sessions of any length. Team ground rules are agreements made by the team members that manage how they will interact, with the aim of continually improving the group's ability to work as a team. They are typically the operating standards that determine how people conduct their discussions and make their decisions. At the beginning of the meeting, the business analyst facilitates a discussion on the ground rules so that the group formulates its own operating standards. The facilitator might ask, "What team operating agreements should we adopt to make our work more efficient and of higher quality?" Or, simply, "What are some important guidelines we should all keep in mind as we work together in this and future meetings?" Use the multivote technique (described in Chapter 4) to gain approval of the rules if there are too many to deal with effectively. The group should review and revise the ground rules as needed. Typical ground rules are listed in Table 2-2.

Table 2-2—Typical Meeting Ground Rules

Ground Rule Item	Suggested Description and Explanation
Meeting management	Team meeting attendance is mandatory. If a member misses a meeting, he or she will take the responsibility to find out what decisions were made and support them or raise issues at the next meeting. If a member must miss a meeting, no delegates are to be sent.
	Team meetings will be conducted on a specific day and time to maintain consistency and facilitate full attendance. Team members are expected to arrive at the meeting on time.
	The facilitator will start and adjourn the meeting on time.
	The facilitator will review the agenda at the start of each meeting and facilitate setting the agenda for the next meeting at the close. Meeting effectiveness will be evaluated at the end of each meeting.
Issue management and conflict resolution	If the team is unable to resolve an issue, the issue will be elevated to the next level of management. Prior to escalation, an analysis of the alternative resolutions will be conducted to formulate recommendations from the group.
Decision-making	Decisions will be made by consensus. Consensus means: "Although this solution might not be my first choice, I can live with the solution—and, therefore, I will support it. And if I can't live with it, it is my responsibility to the group to raise my concerns until they are satisfied."
	Team decisions will be documented and archived.

Carter McNamara has some tips for establishing ground rules.[2] They are presented in Table 2-3.

Table 2-3—Tips for Establishing Ground Rules

Do	Don't
Have a few basic ground rules that can be used for most of your meetings. These ground rules cultivate the basic ingredients needed for a successful meeting.	Develop new ground rules each time you have a meeting.
Establish powerful ground rules, such as participate, get focused, maintain momentum, and reach closure.	Establish too many ground rules.
List your primary ground rules on the agenda.	
If you have new attendees that are not used to your meetings, you might review the ground rules.	Review the ground rules every meeting unless there are a few that are consistently abused.
Keep the ground rules posted at all times.	Establish ground rules once and never refer to them again.
Make sure the participants develop the ground rules so that they own them and are more likely to help the facilitator enforce them.	Develop ground rules yourself.

Conduct the Meeting Using Appropriate Facilitation Techniques

When facilitating the meeting, the business analyst uses the agenda as a powerful tool to stay on track and manage the group's time to achieve the desired outcome. If it appears that an agenda item will take longer than anticipated, the business analyst stops the meeting and explains that the meeting agenda agreed to is in jeopardy. The facilitator does not simply let the time overrun but instead presents the group with these obvious options:

+ Close down the current discussion within a few minutes to move on with the agenda (which is the best option if the matter under discussion is close to closure).

+ Table later agenda items to allow more time to bring the current discussion to closure (which is preferred if further agenda items depend on resolution of the matter at hand).

+ End the discussion and reschedule it on the agenda of a future meeting (which is preferred if there are other, more pressing agenda items).

After the decision is made, the business analyst adjusts the agenda and resumes facilitating the meeting.

During the meeting, a considerable amount of information is verbalized and discussed. The business analyst uses the flip chart as an essential facilitation tool. Chapter 4 presents some tips for using flip charts. The facilitator uses chart writing to:

+ Document the work of the group.

+ Encourage participants to make corrections or ask for clarification.

+ Capture issues, risks, constraints, and assumptions.

+ Park items of interest to become future agenda items; be sure to follow up with these items, or participants will not be motivated to continue their commitment to the effort.

+ Organize the discussion by capturing wording and asking for questions or suggestions, proposing alternatives, combining ideas, depicting consequences, narrowing choices, restating ideas, and summarizing decisions.

Close the Meeting

There are several guidelines for the business analyst to follow when closing sessions:

+ Always close the meeting on time.

+ Review the meeting's purpose, and progress toward achieving meeting objectives.

- Review next steps: disposition of issues, action items, and parked items.

- Set the date, time, and place for the next meeting.

- Evaluate the success of the meeting, using a simple scale of 1–7, where a rating of 7 means expectations were exceeded and 1 means the meeting was ineffective. Quickly go around the room asking for the meeting rating. Note: This is an evaluation of how the group worked together to achieve the meeting's purpose, not of how the facilitator performed.

- Collect lessons learned for meeting improvement; quickly go around the room asking for comments—"What worked well?" "What can we do better for the next meeting?"

Followup after the Meeting

The work accomplished at the meeting often requires a great deal of refinement by the business analyst. Not only does the requirements information need to be captured in a structured, usable manner, but further review and refinement are also likely required to convert the information into mature requirements documentation. An iterative approach to requirements development—short working sessions with speedy information capture and feedback sessions—is the best defense against requirements risks. It is important that the participants involved in creating the requirements also be involved in approving changes and updates to the requirements.

Endnotes

1. Carter McNamara. *Basic Guide to Conducting Effective Meetings*. Online at www.managementhelp.org/misc/mtgmgmnt.htm (accessed August 9, 2007).

2. Ibid.

Chapter 3

Facilitation—It's an Art and a Science

In This Chapter:

- Facilitation versus Subject Matter Expertise
- The Roles and Responsibilities of the Facilitator

What is *facilitation?* Facilitation is different things to different people. We offer the following definitions for consideration. Facilitation is:

+ A process in which an objective meeting chairperson helps a group, composed of people with diverse expertise and styles of interaction, work together effectively to achieve a predetermined outcome

+ A process to foster team collaboration, manage group behaviors, and minimize conflict to accomplish meeting objectives, reach group consensus, or solve identified problems

The *facilitator* focuses on fostering positive group interactions to drive toward a stated goal. Just like the project manager, the business analyst is often thrown into the facilitator's role—that of a group leader or team leader. Business analysts, as a rule, have no decision-making authority. Indeed, their goal is to combine the creative juices of the participants to pull the best decision from the group. The business analyst, however, contributes to the substance of the discussion by asking leading questions, summarizing discussions, and continually testing for consensus. The business analyst as facilitator leads the group process and helps to improve the way the participants communicate, examine and solve problems, and make decisions.[1] Good facilitators help groups stay focused, think outside the box for maximum creativity and innovation, and be more efficient and productive than they would be without expert group process guidance.

Lessons learned through quality assurance practices, the Total Quality Management movement, and the Six Sigma quality measurement and improvement program have shown us that participation is important, teams perform better than individuals, and the team process affects outcomes. It is through the efforts of the skilled facilitator that team performance is optimized. When a group of people come together in a meeting, they are not yet a functioning team. Expert facilitation and team-building techniques are used to quickly convert the participants into a collaborative, high-performing team.

Using expert facilitation skills when conducting requirements elicitation, analysis, specification, and validation sessions has numerous benefits for the business analyst. Table 3-1 offers a list of the benefits of effective facilitation when applied to business analysis.[2]

Table 3-1—Benefits of Using Effective Facilitation

Benefit	Applied to Business Analysis
Motivation	Group members are often motivated to support the decisions made about the requirements for the new business solution because of their investment in the process.
Quality	The best efforts of groups usually produce better business requirements than those developed through individual efforts. Higher-quality decisions normally result.
Full participation	Increased participation within the group increases the creativity and innovation of the requirements. Negative attitudes, low morale, uneven participation, and withholding of information are less likely because everyone is involved in a joint process.

Benefit	Applied to Business Analysis
Team building	Everyone involved has a chance to contribute, and each participant feels like an integral part of the project team.
Ownership	People realize and respect that responsibility for implementing decisions lies with everyone, not just the functional manager, the business analyst, or the project manager.
Skill building	Innovation and problem-solving skills are built into the group, so that the next time they participate in requirements meetings (or any other critical business meeting) they will add more value.
Strategic focus	People are encouraged to think and act for the overall benefit of the organization, not just their department or group.
Conflict management	A forum for constructively resolving requirements conflicts and clarifying misunderstandings is created.

Facilitation Versus Subject Matter Expertise

It is important for the business analyst to be keenly aware of the distinction between *content leadership* and *process leadership*. Content leadership is fulfilled by an expert in the matter under consideration, who usually intends to influence the outcome of the discussion. Process leadership, on the other hand, is performed by a facilitator who directs the group process and encourages the participants to discuss the content and come to consensus on the decision or final outcome. The facilitator provides the structure, methods, and techniques so a group can be free to focus on the content of the issue at hand. Table 3-2 shows the differing perspectives of the two leadership functions.

Table 3-2—Content Focus Versus Process Focus

Content (What) Focus	Process (How) Focus
Topic under discussion	Method to facilitate the topic
The business problem or opportunity	Tools to find solutions
Educating and influencing the group	Rules and guidelines for decisions
The decision	Group activities and dynamics to solve problem and reach consensus
Issues with the decision	Open, honest, and collaborative communications

The Roles and Responsibilities of the Facilitator

The group facilitator uses the facilitation process, tools, and techniques to encourage meeting participants to assume responsibility for the meeting objectives and work collaboratively to produce results. The business analyst performs myriad activities as the group facilitator, including:

+ Developing high-performing teams

+ Leading discussions

+ Planning for success

Developing High-Performing Teams

The Art

It takes a considerable amount of intuition and good old-fashioned gut feeling to build a great team. High-performing teams are unstoppable. Consider the nature of high-performing teams such as surgical, paramedic, firefighter, U.S. Navy SEAL, and NBA basketball teams. What do they have in common? Qualities like those listed below do not come without a considerable amount of leadership and effort. Business analysts and project managers need to learn how to build and sustain high-performing teams to better serve their organizations. High performing teams:

+ Have strong leadership

+ Are multiskilled

+ Are small in number (small, but mighty)

+ Are highly trained and practiced

+ Are passionate about the mission

+ Have clear roles and responsibilities

+ Back up others that need help

+ Help new team members make entry

+ Are driven and do whatever it takes to achieve the goal

+ Help drive discipline into the group

+ Help create a climate of trust

+ Turn diversity to advantage

The business analyst must understand that all teams are groups, but not all groups are teams. Teams are much more effective than groups. An often-used definition of a team put forth by Katzenbach and Smith in *The Wisdom of Teams* is:[3]

> A team is a small number of people with complementary skills who are committed to a common purpose, performance goals, and approach for which they hold themselves mutually accountable.

Today's cross-functional project teams are composed of a set of multiskilled subject matter experts that are brought together because their collective knowledge and proficiencies are needed to create an innovative and integrated solution. It is through this cross-disciplined collaboration that creativity thrives. By their very nature, the multiskilled subject matter experts have widely varying personalities and work styles. It is the facilitator who ensures that the group is effective and that everyone in the group influences decisions. The facilitator encourages team members to leave their titles at the door because power differentials work against team effectiveness. Participants are asked to challenge ideas, accept dispute and questions, and listen to new approaches. The facilitator becomes concerned if ideas are not discussed and challenged sufficiently. The skilled facilitator also models behaviors and coaches team members to act as full, high-performing, and fully committed team members.

The effective facilitator shares the lead and mentors others in the process. The facilitator's leadership role expands and contracts as the team and situation dictate. At the same time, the facilitator is aware not only of where the project is and where it needs to go to achieve its goals but also of where the team is and where it needs to go on its journey from a group to a high-performing team.

There are a multitude of team-building activities, including brief warm-up activities used at the beginning of meetings to get everyone energized and exercises to help teams work through typical team problems. The first and perhaps most valuable team-building activity is preparing for and conducting the first group meeting. At this meeting, the participants are likely to be anxious about what their role will be in the requirements management process and in the overall project. Team-building activities are designed to help the participants work together effectively. Become familiar with an array of team-building activities and use them appropriately but sparingly. Libraries are filled with books that describe team-building exercises of all kinds. One we suggest is *The Team Handbook*, third edition, by Scholtes, Streibel, and Joiner.

The Science

The business analyst does not simply facilitate meetings expertly; she also focuses on building an effective requirements definition and management team to work together throughout the project. In her team-building role, the business analyst:

- Understands group dynamics, manages disruptive behaviors, and leads the group differently depending on the maturity of the team

- Understands individual differences, work styles, and cultural nuances and uses them to the group's advantage

- Provides the foundation for the team to work together by establishing team ground rules and encourages the group to evaluate its progress and establish areas for improvement

- Establishes a sense of trust and ethics among team members

When the business analyst is facilitating a group, it is helpful to understand team dynamics and team development models and to know how to guide the team through the early formation stages to the high-performing stage as quickly as possible. Many models of team development are available for study and guidance. The most widely used is Bruce Tuchman's stages of team development, depicted in Figure 3-1. This model serves as a guide for taking into account the development issues that could cause dilemmas for the business analyst and the project manager. The model demonstrates that team maturation is dynamic and that the team is constantly adjusting to new input into the team. For example, when a new member joins the team, the team might revert back to the early formative stages for a time. In fact, all team development stages are always present to some degree, though one tends to be dominant. At each stage the business analyst has a certain role to play to maximize team effectiveness.

Figure 3-1—Team Development Stages

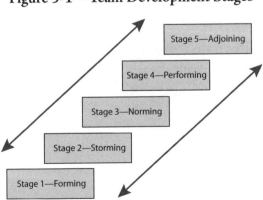

Refer to *From Analyst to Leader: Elevating the Role of the Business Analyst*, another book in the Business Analysis Essentials Library, for a detailed discussion of team development.

It is also important for the business analyst to understand the body of work that defines the diverse personalities and preferred work styles of individuals, referred to as psychological types. Only then can the business analyst help the group to embrace differing work styles and optimize the value of each participant. One commonly used instrument, based on a theory of human personality that is based on the work of Swiss psychiatrist Carl G. Jung and further refined by Katherine Cook Briggs and Isabel Briggs Myers, is the Myers-Briggs Type Indicator® (MBTI®). The theory proposes that human behavior is not random but instead follows identifiable patterns that develop from the structure of the human mind. The MBTI® helps people understand their preferences for:

+ Energy

+ Information gathering

+ Decision-making

+ Orientation to the outer world (lifestyle)

The MBTI® is a self-report questionnaire designed to make Carl Jung's theory of psychological types understandable and useful in everyday life, and it is invaluable when applied to groups of individuals working in teams. The MBTI® is a measure of personality, not intelligence, aptitude, or achievement. It measures a person's preferred way of thinking or behaving. The MBTI® reports preferences on the four dichotomies (preference scales):

Extraversion (E)   OR   Introversion (I)

Sensing (S)   OR   Intuition (N)

Thinking (T)   OR   Feeling (F)

Judging (J)   OR   Perceiving (P)

Leading Discussions

Perhaps the most important facilitator role for the business ana-lyst is directing discussions to drive the group toward the best deci-sion. Toward that end, the business analyst uses various facilitation techniques to achieve these goals:

+ Foster a climate conducive to participative decision-making, dialogue, and interaction

+ Provide structure and guidance to help the group achieve its goals

+ Actively listen and periodically summarize discussion points, focusing on areas of agreement

+ Define the focus of the team and modify the team focus when needed

The Art

The successful business analyst becomes quite skilled at directing communication in groups. Mastering the art of leading discussions requires one to jump in head first and gain valuable experience. Several of the techniques discussed in the next chapter—including the art of asking pointed questions and how to listen, summarize, and reframe ideas—are learned and polished only through experience.

The Science

Many theories about communication and communication models are designed to ensure that communication occurs optimally. Communication has many dimensions:

+ Written and oral—listening and speaking

+ Internal and external—within the project and to the customer and other external stakeholders

+ Formal and informal—reports, briefings, and reviews; memos, conversations, and email

+ Vertical and horizontal—up and down and with peers

To successfully lead discussions, the business analyst hones her skills at listening and speaking and leading informal group discussions. Group discussions led by the business analyst must always be purposeful and intentional.

When planning the discussion approach, it is helpful to be mindful of different communication categories.

+ **Acknowledgment.** This type of communication takes place when you let people know that you see or hear them, as you nod, or when you rephrase a comment to confirm that you have understood the message.

+ **Questioning.** This type takes place by asking or inquiring about the content under discussion, but beware: if the question is not stated carefully, it can be interpreted as a challenge.

+ **Providing feedback.** Through pointed questions or declarative sentences, give speakers your impressions of their comments. Feedback must be crafted with careful consideration for those with whom you are communicating.

- **Teaching, instructing, or guiding.** In requirements elicitation meetings, some training takes place and information is provided. Keep the training informal and brief.

- **Ordering or directing.** Use this type of communication only in extreme situations, when a decision must be made immediately.

- **Bad faith.** This message is consciously or unconsciously directed at being disruptive, negative, or inappropriately critical. The facilitator must become skilled at managing disruptive behaviors.

- **Play.** Even at work, we communicate messages of play—joking. Humor is a wonderful strategy to break tensions and reduce stress as the team does its work.

Often when communication is not clear, it is because people are not clear about the type of message. You might feel that someone is asking for information, but instead that person might actually be presenting a strong message. In this case, the interaction might get off track and the message might get lost. Start over and clarify the purpose. Call a time out, and walk through the discussion slowly and carefully.

The next chapter presents some of the approaches most often used when facilitating group discussions, and it provides a host of tools and techniques to become a masterful discussion leader. Refer to *From Analyst to Leader: Elevating the Role of the Business Analyst* for a detailed discussion on communication.

Planning for Success

The business analyst does not facilitate the requirements definition and management process alone. Rather, the business analyst collaborates with the project manager, the technical lead, and the business visionary to plan and execute the requirements activities. To ensure success, the business analyst:

+ Develops and plans for requirements activities in collaboration with core team members

+ Secures commitment from management of the business units and the performing organization for the resources needed to complete the requirements activities

+ Designs and plans the sequence and timing of requirements elicitation, analysis, specification, documentation, and validation meetings

+ Periodically conducts lessons learned sessions to continually improve the collaborative approach to requirements definition and management

The Art

The business analyst works in close collaboration with the project manager and other key team members to plan the requirements definition and management activities. To master the art of planning, your project manager is your best resource. In addition, the general techniques discussed in the previous chapter will help you to plan any meeting you will lead.

The Science

The science of planning is covered in detail in the Project Management Institute's *A Guide to the Project Management Body of Knowledge*, third edition (*PMBOK® Guide*)[4] and the vast array of project management books and classes in the marketplace. The business analyst benefits from becoming a generalist in the art and science of project management. Again, to understand the science of planning and apply it to organizing your requirements activities, your project manager is your best resource. In addition, the detailed discussions in later chapters of this book will help you to plan the specific meetings facilitated by the business analyst.

Endnotes

1. Roger M. Schwartz. *The Skilled Facilitator: Practical Wisdom for Developing Effective Groups*, 1994. San Francisco: Jossey-Bass.

2. Brad Spangler. "Facilitatation," *Beyond Intractability*, 2003. Online at www.beyondintractability.org/essay/facilitation (accessed August 10, 2007). Spangler cites Fran Rees, *The Facilitator Excellence Handbook* (Jossey-Bass, 1998) in his article.

3. Jon R. Katzenbach and Douglas K. Smith. *The Wisdom of Teams*, 1993. Boston: Harvard Business School Press.

4. Project Management Institute. *A Guide to the Project Management Body of Knowledge*, 3rd ed., 2004. Newtown Square, PA: Project Management Institute, Inc.

Chapter 4

The Business Analyst's Facilitation Toolkit

In This Chapter:

- Group Analysis Skills

- Group Communication Skills

- Group Process Skills

Brad Spangler specifies the skills required of an effective facilitator:[1]

Facilitators must have a variety of skills and techniques to be effective. Strong verbal and analytical skills are essential. Facilitators must know what questions to ask, when to ask them, and how questions should be structured to get good answers without defensiveness. Facilitators must know how to probe for more information when the initial answers are not sufficient. They must also know how to rephrase or "reframe" statements to enhance understanding, and to highlight areas of agreement and disagreement as they develop.

Other skills include redirecting questions and comments, giving positive reinforcement, encouraging contrasting views, including quieter members of the group, and dealing with domineering or hostile participants. Nonverbal techniques include things such as eye contact, attentiveness, facial expressions, body language, enthusiasm, and maintaining a positive outlook. A facilitator must also develop the ability to read and analyze group dynamics on the spot in order to guide the group in a productive way.

According to Miranda Duncan, effective meeting facilitation requires skill in three areas:[2]

+ Analysis

  □ Separating content from process

  □ Identifying interests

  □ Framing problems or opportunities

+ Communication

  □ Choice of words

  □ Ability to listen, summarize, and reframe

  □ Using questions to stimulate thinking and control the process

+ Group process models

  □ Group leadership

  □ Decision-making and consensus-building

  □ Keeping the meeting on track

The remaining sections of this chapter explore the facilitation skills required to successfully perform as a competent business analyst and suggest using the most-often-used tools and techniques to apply when facilitating groups.

Group Analysis Skills

Before making decisions, the group almost always needs to conduct a certain amount of analysis. The business analyst as facilitator leads the group through a process to define the problem or opportunity at hand, identify options, determine criteria by which to evaluate the effectiveness of each option, apply the criteria to each option, and step back and look at the data. Only after discussing the pros and cons of each option should the group make a decision. *Until the group performs the analysis, it should not focus on or commit to any specific plan of action on the content.* The business analyst as facilitator encourages the group to understand and separate the process from the content and prompts the group to determine the process to analyze the business problem or opportunity first and then move on to the goal or content issues. Analyzing involves:

+ Separating content from process

+ Identifying interests

+ Framing problems or opportunities

Separating Content from Process

As previously noted, it is imperative for the business analyst to fully understand the art and power of facilitation so as to remain objective and not unduly influence the group's decisions. The skilled facilitator focuses on what the meeting is about, the subject or issue at hand, and analysis of the content. In the business analyst's world, the *content* of a typical requirements elicitation meeting is the definition of the business need and the *process* is how the business analyst works with the group to define the business need accurately and analyze it completely. The business analyst provides opportunities for content experts to present information and influence group decisions. The subject matter expert likely uses a presentation style to impart his expertise. Conversely, the business analyst likely uses a facilitating style to confirm and validate the information and to seek input from others as to their perspectives. There is a distinct dichotomy between a *presentation leadership style* and a *facilitating leadership style*, as demonstrated in Table 4-1.[3]

Table 4-1—Presentation Style versus Facilitating Style

Presentation Style	Facilitating Style
Mostly one-way communication	Multiple-way communication
Presentation format	Participation format
Tell-and-sell approach	Problem-solving approach
Ideas presented and defended	Ideas generated by group members
Suitable for passing on information	Suitable for productive group work
Limits on group creativity	Maximization of group creativity

Identifying Interests

Another critical analytic skill is the ability to recognize an underlying interest and bring it out into the open so it can be discussed and negotiated. For instance, a key subject matter expert (SME) might not want to discuss a particular agenda item with the full group, claiming it is an unnecessary drain on time and resources. The underlying interest, however, might be that the SME does not want to be embarrassed by his lack of progress on the issue. The facilitator should respect the validity of the SME's reluctance to push forward with the discussion by asking questions such as: "How can we involve the members of the requirements definition team without the meeting degrading?" Once group analysis techniques are put into place to prevent his being discredited, the SME will be quite willing to involve the team in the analysis and decision as to how to move forward.

Framing Problems or Opportunities

Business problems and opportunities must be stated clearly and analyzed sufficiently prior to drafting requirements for the business solution. The problem/opportunity statement is worded without bias so that participants with differing viewpoints accept the description.

Framing business problems. If the project has been commissioned to solve a business problem, steps typically include the following:

1. Document the problem in as much detail as possible.

2. Determine the adverse impacts the problem is causing within the organization; quantify the impacts in terms of lost revenue, inefficiencies, etc.

3. Determine the immediacy of the resolution and the cost of doing nothing.

4. Conduct root cause analysis to determine the underlying source of the issues.

5. Determine the potential areas of analysis required to address the issues.

6. Draft a requirements statement describing the business need for a solution.

Framing business opportunities. If the project has been commissioned to take advantage of a new business opportunity, steps typically include the following:

1. Define the opportunity in as much detail as possible; include the events that led up to the discovery of the opportunity and the business benefits expected if the opportunity is pursued.

2. Quantify the expected benefits in terms of increased revenue, reduced costs, etc.

3. Determine the immediacy of the resolution and the cost of doing nothing.

4. Identify the opportunity cost of pursuing this opportunity versus another being considered.

5. Determine the approach to be undertaken to complete the analysis required to understand the viability of the opportunity.

6. Draft a requirements statement describing the business need for a solution.

Analysis Techniques

As the business analyst facilitates the group in defining business problems and opportunities and presenting, describing, analyzing, refining, and validating the requirements under consideration, several tools and techniques are commonly used, including:

- Facilitated discussions
- Presentations
- Break-out groups
- Flip charts
- Storyboards
- Gap analysis
- SWOT (strengths, weaknesses, opportunities, and threats) analysis

Facilitated Discussions

The power of the facilitator lies in the ability to draw out the knowledge and expertise of participants, encourage creativity and innovation, and drive the group to the best decision using the skills presented here. Typical guidelines to facilitate effective discussions include:[4]

+ Prepare for the discussion

+ Open the discussion

+ Listen intently

+ Ask for clarification

+ Manage participation

+ Summarize the discussion

+ Manage time

+ Corral digressions

+ Close the discussion

Presentations

As we have discovered, presentations are typically one-way communication. They are, however, essential to the group process to level set the group. Persons within the group that have less information than others feel at a disadvantage and, as a result, might shut down. The facilitator plans the use of presentations delivered by selected subject matter experts carefully. The meeting will begin to degrade if presentations are too lengthy or mired in detail. Be sure to allow time for a facilitated discussion after the presentation for the group to process the information and understand its relevance to the meeting objectives.

In addition, the business analyst might be called upon to give presentations on the status of the requirements activities. Giving an effective presentation can often determine the level of continued support for the effort. The business analyst may present requirement status to the project team, the project sponsor, members of management, or members of the customer group. To create an effective presentation, the business analyst would be wise to follow the steps below. Be brief and concise, and remember the Golden Rule: tell them what you are going to tell them, tell them, and summarize what you have told them.[5]

1. Assess listener needs.

2. Write a clear purpose of the presentation.

3. Develop three or four main points.

4. Create visuals.

5. Organize the sequence.

6. Develop an introduction.

7. Write a summary and conclusions.

Break-Out Groups

When planning large meetings and workshops, the business analyst should consider using break-out groups for small teams to work together, capture their ideas on their own flip charts, and report back to the full group of participants. If you have all the break-out groups work on the same issue or question, you will see themes emerge from the different groups during the out-brief, thus revealing the consensus thinking of the group. If you have the break-out groups work on different issues and have concurrent work going on, you can quickly gather information on several different topics. During the break-out group out-briefs, be sure to facilitate a discussion and capture the additional thinking of the entire group.

Flip Charts

Skilled use of this low-tech tool is perhaps the most essential business analysis skill. There is power in the act of recording a person's idea and allowing the group to ask questions for clarity, refine the idea for improvement, and build on it to add value and creativity to the concept. As this process ensues, the idea becomes owned by the group, not only its originator. As ideas are captured on flip charts and posted around the room, the participants begin to see how productive they have been, which is motivating and energizing.

The flip chart information serves as the output of the meeting. After the meeting, the business analyst works with the meeting scribe to capture all the information created by the team into the first iteration of requirements documentation. Here are some simple suggestions for using flip charts effectively:

- Learn to write legibly and neatly across the paper (lined paper helps); print rather than writing in cursive.

- Use color to help distinguish between ideas.

- Number ideas for ease of discussion.

- Use the sticky type of flip chart paper to avoid having to use tape to post the flip chart sheets on the wall.

- Listen carefully to the idea being presented, summarize it in a brief phrase, and ask the originator if what you have recorded accurately describes the idea.

+ Once you have captured the idea to the satisfaction of the originator, ask the group for questions, comments, and recommendations; encourage the group to add to the idea.

+ Do not change the verbiage of the idea presented without the originator's permission because doing so might alter the intended meaning.

+ Ask questions for clarity if you do not understand the idea (if you don't understand it, others are likely to be confused as well).

Storyboards

Storyboards are an effective way to document group work in a manner that is easily followed and graphically interesting. A storyboard is a series of panels used to depict elements of a project or process. Initially developed by Walt Disney Studios, storyboards are used extensively in the film industry to depict scenes, copy, and shots for commercials and movies. They are also used extensively in the engineering arena to accompany project proposals. The project manager often uses storyboards as a series of diagrams and text to show how a project to develop a new business solution will look.

The business analyst could use the storyboard in two ways. The first is to describe the steps in the requirements elicitation, analysis, specification, documentation, and validation processes, using one box for each major activity. Each box would contain some text explaining the purpose of the activity, measures of success, deliverables, and schedule, and would be accompanied by a graphical depiction of the process, output, or both (see Figure 4-1 for an example). The second use of storyboards is as a powerful communication tool during requirement review meetings, providing a visual summary of business requirements captured to date. Storyboards might indeed become the first iteration of requirements documentation. Tips for creating a storyboard can be seen in Table 4-2, and a sample storyboard can be seen in Figure 4-1.

Figure 4-1—Example of a Storyboard

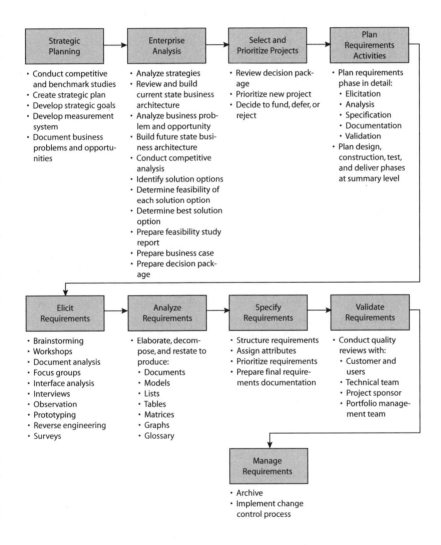

Table 4-2—Tips for Creating a Storyboard

Do	Don't
Keep the text brief	Use long or complex verbiage
Use lots of visuals	Make the visuals too complex
Construct the storyboard in a flowchart style accompanied by a sequence of boxed information	Make the storyboard too long
Make sure each box represents a major step in the business function or process	Get too detailed with the first iteration

Gap Analysis

The gap analysis is a valuable business analysis tool. A gap analysis can be used to:

+ Benchmark or otherwise assess general expectation of performance in industry, compared with current organizational capabilities.

+ Determine, document, and evaluate the variance or distance between the current and desired future business process.

+ Determine, document, and approve the variance between business requirements and system capabilities in terms of commercial off-the-shelf (COTS) packaged application features (also referred to as a deficiency assessment).

+ Discover discrepancies between two or more sets of diagrams.

+ Analyze the gap between requirements that are met and those not met (again, referred to as a deficiency assessment).

+ Compare actual performance against potential performance, and then determine the areas that need improvement.

The steps to conduct a gap analysis are typically:

1. Describe the current state of the business process undergoing change. This is often accomplished by developing a storyboard, a process flowchart, or a workflow diagram.

2. Describe the future state of the business process.

3. Compare the current state with the future state.

4. Document the changes (gaps) needed to get from the current to the future state.

SWOT Analysis

A SWOT analysis is a valuable tool to quickly analyze various aspects of the current state of the business process undergoing change. The steps are as follows:

1. Draw a grid similar to the one in Figure 4-2.

2. Describe the issue or problem under discussion at the top of the grid.

3. Conduct a brainstorming session (described in detail later in this chapter) to complete each section in the grid.

4. Facilitate a discussion to analyze the results. Remember that the group has identified only potential characteristics of the problem. Further analysis is needed to validate the actual characteristics, ideally confirmed with data.

5. Once the characteristics of the issue or problem have been validated, the group brainstorms potential solutions to solve the problem.

Figure 4-2—SWOT Chart

<Problem Description>

Strengths	Weaknesses
Opportunities	Threats

Force Field Analysis

Force field analysis is a powerful tool used by a facilitator to identify and address driving and restraining factors when solving a problem or implementing organizational change. Once a team has selected an option, this tool focuses the team on implementation issues. Typically, the business analyst facilitates a brainstorming session to identify forces that will help or hinder implementing the selected option. After this list is generated, the business analyst combines like ideas, prioritizes them, and develops actions to deal with key forces. To develop the force field analysis:

1. Write the idea (problem or planned change) on a flip chart or white board.

2. Draw two columns below the idea; label the left column "driving forces" and the right column "restraining forces," similar to the sample shown in Figure 4-3.

Figure 4-3—Force Field Analysis Diagram

Title

Status Quo	Desired Outcome
(enter status quo here)	(enter desired outcome here)
Driving Forces	Restraining Forces
(enter driving forces here)	(enter restraining forces here)

3. Brainstorm forces in each column; encourage creativity.

4. Determine which restraining forces could be removed or weakened and which driving forces can be strengthened.

Force field diagrams can also be used to list pros and cons, strengths and weaknesses, what is known and what is unknown, and perceptions of parties in conflict and to compare the current and target situations.

Root Cause Analysis

Root cause analysis uses a structured process to identify a problem, gather information, identify and chart root causes, generate recommendations, and develop an action plan to take corrective action. Two techniques are most commonly used, the *cause-and-effect diagram,* also referred to as the *Ishikawa* or *fishbone diagram,* and the *five whys.*

When using a team approach to problem solving, it is helpful to capture the team's brainstorming on root causes visually. A cause-and-effect diagram is used to identify and organize the possible causes of a problem. This tool helps the group to focus on the cause of the problem instead of the solution. The technique organizes ideas for further analysis. The diagram serves as a map depicting possible cause-and-effect relationships (refer to Figure 4-4 for an example of a cause-and-effect diagram). Steps to develop a cause-and-effect diagram include:

1. Capture the issue or problem under discussion in a box at the top of the diagram.

2. Draw a line from the box across the paper or white board (forming the spine of the fishbone).

3. Draw diagonal lines from the spine to represent categories of potential causes of the problem. The categories may include people, process, tools, and policies.

4. Draw smaller lines to represent deeper causes.

5. Brainstorm categories and potential causes of the problem and capture them under the appropriate category.

6. Analyze the results. Remember that the group has identified only potential causes of the problem. Further analysis is needed to validate the actual cause, ideally with data.

7. Brainstorm potential solutions once the actual cause has been identified.

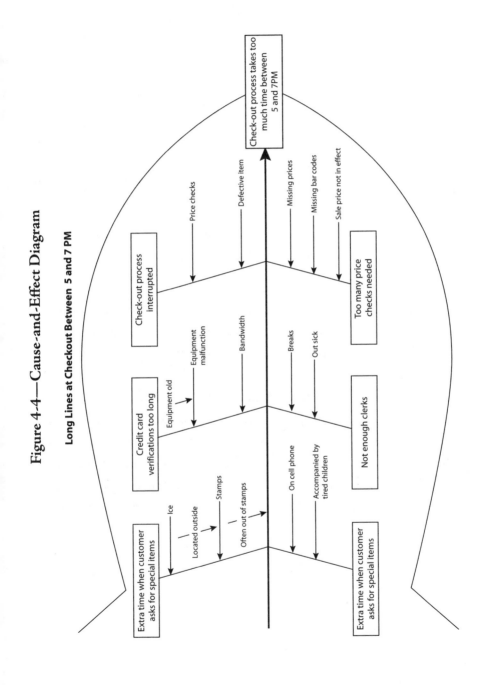

Figure 4-4—Cause-and-Effect Diagram

Long Lines at Checkout Between 5 and 7 PM

The five whys approach repeatedly asks questions in an attempt to get to the root cause of the problem. The five whys is one of the simplest facilitation tools to use when problems have a human interaction component. To use this technique:

1. Write the problem on a flip chart or white board.

2. Ask "Why do you think this problem occurs?" and capture the idea below the problem.

3. Ask "Why?" again and capture that idea below the first idea.

4. Continue with Step 3 until you are convinced the actual root cause has been identified. This may take more or less than five questions.

The five whys can be used alone or as part of the fishbone diagram technique. After all ideas are captured in the diagram, use the five whys approach to drill down to the root causes.

Group Communication Skills

Communication skills are discussed in detail in numerous books and papers. Refer to *From Analyst to Leader: Elevating the Role of the Business Analyst* for a detailed discussion of communication skills. In this book we focus on the following important business analysis communication techniques that are used when leading discussions:

+ Choose words carefully.

+ Listen, summarize, and reframe.

+ Ask pointed questions.

Choose Words Carefully

It is important for the business analyst to be knowledgeable about the culture and politics of the organization. In some groups, unfortunate words, so-called *red-letter words*, can cause powerful emotions because of past occurrences. The business analyst can use certain strategies to avoid inciting negative feelings due to an unfortunate choice of wording:

- ✦ Familiarize yourself with the business and technical areas as much as possible.

- ✦ Ask questions and patiently listen for the entire answer.

- ✦ Actively seek input from the participants.

- ✦ Encourage questions and different opinions.

- ✦ Reframe and restate information, choosing your wording carefully.

- ✦ Refrain from changing the words the participants used unless the words are ambiguous.

- ✦ Encourage participants to take ownership of issues, ambiguities, problems, and selection of the appropriate terminology.

Listen, Summarize, and Reframe

To ensure that effective communication is occurring, the business analyst predominantly relies on listening intently, summarizing, restating, and asking questions to progressively elaborate requirements. As the discussion unfolds, the business analyst replays the message back to the group for clarity and understanding and captures the key points on a flip chart for all to see, review, and refine. Referring to the flip chart, the business analyst summarizes the discussion that has occurred thus far, asks for approval of the wording, and encourages the group to move on. This technique is particularly useful when the group begins to digress. Alternatively, the business analyst can ask someone in the group to summarize. Then the group moves on to the next planned agenda item or activity.

Ask Pointed Questions

The value of asking pointed questions during meetings cannot be overstated. For the business analyst to become skilled at asking good questions, she must be well acquainted with both the business domain and the technical nomenclature used in the organization.

According to Duncan, asking leading and challenging questions is the most powerful facilitation technique for controlling the discussion and stimulating innovation. Duncan writes that a well-formed question is invaluable because it:[6]

- *Signals progress by showing that the group is launching into its agenda: "Shall we begin?" "What do you hope to walk away with by the end of the meeting?"*

- *Brings the discussion back on track: "Shall we add that topic to the agenda for next time?" "Do we need to make sure we cover the other items before we run out of time?" Or, "Do we need to decide this in order to decide that?" Questions can provide closure: "Is there anything else before we move on?" "What are our next steps?"*

- *Stimulates thinking and rethinking. Statements can be perceived as, or actually are, challenges provoking a counter-challenge or assertion of a superior idea. Questions, on the other hand, create a temporary vacuum—a time for reflection.*

- *Eliminates much of the superfluous posturing and maintains an air of openness, an attitude of, "Let me hear more before I decide."*

Examples: "If you do this, what will happen?" "Could you describe the process of communication you currently use?" "If you could change one thing about this requirement, what would it be?" In other words, questions, rather than directives or advice, are the most potent way to encourage the group to focus on something, rethink a course of action, or evaluate options.

Questions are structured to accomplish a specific goal. The business analyst may formulate a question to define the scope of the problem, gather data about the problem, and finally begin to draft requirements to solve the problem. Questions are also used to assess an issue or to plan the approach to the discussion. Questions not only promote participation from everyone equally but also manage the discussion. Facilitators often use questions to resolve group dysfunctions, identify the true problem, uncover hidden agendas, and finally drive to consensus. The expert facilitator selects the questioning technique depending on the situation:

- *Probing* questions to dive deeper into an idea

- *Floating* ideas to encourage brainstorming and innovation

- *Prompting* to push an idea further—to think it through

- *Summarizing or reframing* a concept to reinforce the idea and ensure a common understanding

- *Redirecting* the conversation to bring the group back on track

- *Focusing* questions, also to bring the group back to the agenda item under review

- *Facilitating commitment* and ensuring that consensus has been reached

Table 4-3 presents a few tips for using questions to control the meeting discussion and drive the group to consensus.

Table 4-3—Tips to Control Meeting Discussion

Do	Don't
Test controversial questions on some participants in advance	Ask the foolish question to get the answer you want
Ask open-ended and context-free questions	Ask questions that avoid the true issue
Begin with broad questions to establish the topic and ask follow-up questions to narrow the topic	Ask questions that are not aligned with the meeting objectives
Plan in advance the questions to be asked for each topic	Ask questions that put participants on the defensive
Plan questions appropriate for your audience	Direct questions to the participants that are dominating the meeting

Group Process Skills

Group process skills are an invaluable asset that professional facilitators bring to meetings. As we have discussed, productive meetings require structure and attention to process. We will examine the role of the facilitator in the following essential group process activities:

+ Group leadership

+ Group decision-making

+ Group focus: keeping the meeting on track

Group Leadership

Facilitating groups through effective meetings involves motivating the group by encouraging maximum involvement of all participants. The effective meeting facilitator knows the difference between controlling a group and facilitating a group. Fran Rees clearly states the business analyst's goals when facilitating requirements elicitation and validation meetings: "The goal is not to gain power but to complete the work assigned to the team. The goal is not to divide power into definable pieces but to work together to produce what could not be produced by individuals working alone."[7]

Team Facilitation

The business analyst's facilitation role is different from that of an external professional facilitator brought into an organization to facilitate a single meeting. The external facilitator attempts to understand the audience but is not focused on the development of the team's maturity. On the other hand, the business analyst works as an integral part of a project team throughout the business solution life cycle (BSLC). In this role, the business analyst is well suited to assist the project leadership team in becoming a high-performing team, as discussed in the previous chapter. In addition, the savvy business analyst will alter her facilitation style based on the current state of the group.

Team Leadership

An understanding of the importance of team leadership skills for business analysts is emerging. It is now considered appropriate for the business analyst to only *be aware* of the technical area of the project, not to be the technical expert. The business analyst's project focus is on business, rather than technical, objectives. The business analyst understands that projects are technical solutions to business problems that are solved with human intervention and collaboration. Behavioral, people skills are now considered vital for project success.

To complement the team development model presented in the previous chapter, David C. Kolb, Ph.D., offers a five-stage team development model.[8] The value of the model is that it describes the ideal facilitator style for each stage of team development. The facilitator learns to adopt a certain role to maximize team effectiveness. Kolb contends that a group facilitator subtly alters her style of meeting facilitation depending on the group's composition and level of maturity. While continually using basic facilitation skills, the business analyst complements them with mediation, coaching, consulting, and collaborating styles to lead discussions as needed. The experienced facilitator moves seamlessly between these facilitation modes as she observes and diagnoses the team's performance. The business analyst needs to work to acquire all the team leadership roles mentioned in Table 4-4 and, more important, to know when and how to apply them, because teams dynamically move in and out of development phases during the life of the project. To learn more details about the Kolb model, refer to *From Analyst to Leader: Elevating the Role of the Business Analyst*, another book in this series.

Table 4-4—Five-Stage Team Development Model

Development Phase	Facilitator Role
Building	Facilitator
Learning	Mediator
Trusting	Coach
Working	Consultant
Flowing	Collaborator

Group Decision-Making

Virtually all group participants will be most familiar and comfortable with making decisions by voting. Voting is appropriate to some situations but is almost never appropriate in the business environment, where decisions are made on the basis of business value to the enterprise as a whole. This is because of the all or nothing, win/lose outcome of decisions by voting. So, when is it appropriate for a facilitator to make decisions based on a vote? Only when the facilitator finds herself in the situation where there has been ample dialogue; the participants are large in number, diverse, and geographically dispersed; and time is of the essence and it is imperative to make a decision and move on.

Several decision-making options are depicted in Table 4-5. Selecting the appropriate approach will make the decision-making process more likely to succeed.

Table 4-5—Decision-Making Options

Decision Type	Appropriate When
Total agreement	◆ Full discussion is not required and everyone is united on the issue
Assigned decision	◆ One person will take full responsibility for the decision and is accountable for the results
Voting	◆ Options are presented by the stakeholders and a division of the group as a result of the vote is acceptable
Compromise	◆ Opposite views prevent a decision and a middle position incorporating ideas from both sides is developed
Consensus	◆ Buy-in of all affected stakeholders is essential

Consensus Decision-Making

Consensus decision-making is the most-often-used approach for teams defining requirements. Clearly, in a business environment where decisions should be made based on business value to the enterprise as a whole, the facilitator's job is to drive the group to consensus. There is a great deal of confusion about what consensus decision-making is and what it is not. Consensus is reached when debate has taken place, the interests of all participants have been considered, and a decision has been made *and will be supported by everyone.*

Consensus does not mean that the decision is necessarily everyone's first choice. It does mean that everyone can live with it and commits to supporting it. If the decision did not come easily, the facilitator probes further by explaining that if anyone still has reservations about the decision, she has the responsibility to raise the issue to the group for further discussion before the final decision is made and the discussion is closed. In effect, everyone has veto power and should use it until she can truly support the decision in the future. Consensus means that all considerations have been discussed and resolved. For very important decisions, the facilitator polls the group one by one, posing the question: "Can you live with it and will you support it?"

Consensus decision-making is difficult for newly formed teams, the members of which have not yet begun to trust one another. The skilled facilitator, however, uses the consensus-building process to unite the group, uncover various perspectives, and foster a collaborative approach to decisions to improve buy-in. When making decisions, use the consensus approach when a large number of stakeholders sense that they are positively or negatively affected by the decision. Be sure to allow adequate time for discussion to understand various perspectives and positions on the problem, and to resolve valid concerns. When consensus cannot be met, the facilitator must determine the next best way to handle the decision from among other alternatives. In most cases, if consensus was required, the facilitator escalates the issue to the next level of management for resolution. Presented in Table 4-6 are a few tips for making decisions by consensus.

Table 4-6—Consensus Decision-Making

Do	Don't
Set the stage; put the decision in the context of the big picture, and the mission and objective of the project.	Start the process until it is clear what decision needs to be made and why.
Ensure that everyone has adequate information: "What additional questions do you have about the issue?" "What areas are unclear?"	Start the process until the participants have been level set with the same information.
Write the decision to be made on a flip chart for all to see.	Overlook the possibility that everyone might not understand the question in the same way.
Draft decision criteria; then test each decision option against the criteria.	Make important decisions without drafting criteria for acceptance and ensuring that all participants agree with the criteria.

Do	Don't
Capture agreements to parts of the decision to encourage additional collaboration: "Well, we all agree on these points."	Focus on the differences of the group.
Ask for forces working for and against the decision: "Let's really explore the potential results of this decision in various scenarios."	Shut down discussion too early; consensus takes time.
Continue to encourage creativity and innovation in the solution: "Isn't there something else we can do to make this work?"	Allow the decision to be made if even one participant cannot support it; continue to explore that person's reservations until they have been removed: "You have a valid concern. Let's all work to resolve it."

Once the decision is made, the facilitator moves quickly to action. Implementation strategies include:

+ Assign an owner or person responsible for acting on the decision.

+ Identify activities and tasks that will support the decision, and work with the project manager to identify resource requirements, timelines, and associated costs.

+ Determine whether there are any communication or training requirements during the implementation of the decision.

Decision-Making Tools and Techniques

Depending on the type of meeting, effective tools can bring about the best group decision to solve a problem or identify the best alternative. Most of these are used during informal working sessions and formal workshops.

Surveys

Distributing a quick questionnaire about the issue to relevant stakeholders often helps to uncover facts and opinions. This technique is useful when there is a significant amount of unknown information. A survey can gather important information quickly. To help drive to the decision, ask questions such as:

+ What are the differing opinions?

+ Who is involved or affected?

+ Why does the issue exist?

+ When does the decision need to be made?

+ What are the possible options or alternatives?

+ Are there any unrepresented views? Was someone not included in the meeting?

Brainstorming

Brainstorming is perhaps the most-often-used facilitation technique. Brainstorming is a technique for generating a list of ideas about an issue. It promotes innovation, creativity, and out-of-the-box thinking. Before teams make a decision, they should make sure they have examined as broad a range of options as possible. Brainstorming is an easy, enjoyable, and effective way to generate a list of ideas. It truly is a "group brain dump." This is the process business analysts use most often to promote team involvement, so learn to do it well.

Brainstorming is used to generate lists of problems, issues, ideas, solutions, and items. The facilitator works to make the session quick and enjoyable, generate excitement, and stimulate involvement. A successful brainstorming session lets people be as imaginative as possible and does not restrict creativity in any way. This technique is used to equalize participant involvement. It often results in original solutions to problems. Refer to another volume in this series, *Unearthing Business Requirements: Elicitation Tools and Techniques*, for additional information about brainstorming.

Brainstorming Guidelines

+ Encourage everyone to get into the spirit. Don't hold back on any ideas, even if they seem silly at the time; the more ideas the better.

+ Do not allow any discussion during the brainstorming session. Explain that there will be time for discussion later; the goal now is to identify as many ideas as possible.

+ No judgment is allowed. No one is allowed to criticize another person's ideas—not even with a groan or a grimace. (Note: People don't usually understand this rule, but it is imperative that no one renders judgment on the ideas as they are presented. Sometimes the wildest idea is the best.)

+ Encourage people to build on ideas generated by others in the group.

+ Write all ideas on a flip chart so the whole group can easily scan them.

Brainstorming Sequence of Events

+ **Clarify purpose.** The facilitator reviews the purpose of the brainstorming session. Write the question on a flip chart or white board, or hand out sheets of paper with the question on them. This way, people can refer back to the question when they want to be reminded of the session's purpose.

+ **Generate ideas.** Give everyone a minute or two of silence to think about ideas. Ask them to jot their ideas down as they come to mind. Ask them to try to think of at least three to five items.

♦ **List ideas.** Go around the room asking each participant for his or her best idea. As you facilitate, enforce the ground rules ("No discussion! Next idea..." Discussion limits creativity.) Write all ideas on the flip chart, or collect and post them if sticky notes are used. Be sure to number each idea. Pause only to check for accuracy. (The scribe may not change the wording unless the presenter agrees.) Encourage participants to build on each other's ideas. This is when the creativity begins to come into play. Continue until everyone's list is complete.

♦ **Clarify and combine.** The facilitator asks if anyone has questions of clarity about any items listed. The person who contributed the idea should be the one to answer questions, but others may join in. The wording may be changed for clarification but only when the person who originally proposed the idea agrees. See if ideas can be combined. Renumber, assigning the same number to like ideas. Ask the members of the group to write down the numbers of the items they would like addressed or selected. Tally the votes. You may do this by letting members vote by a show of hands as each item number is called out, or ask the participants to use markers and put checkmarks beside their top three choices.

♦ **Prioritize.** To reduce the list, eliminate the items with the fewest votes. The objective is to get no more than five to eight ideas. The rule of thumb is this: if it is a small group (5 or fewer members), cross off items with only 1 or 2 votes; if it is a medium group (6 to 15), eliminate anything with 3 or fewer votes; if it is large group (more than 15), eliminate items with 4 votes or fewer.

♦ **Discuss and refine.** If time allows, you may discuss and refine the wording of the remaining ideas. Be sure to be clear what the next steps will be: What are we now going to do with the prioritized list of ideas?

Brainstorming Variations

+ **Brainwriting.** Brainwriting, also referred to as the *knowledge café*, is a tool for small groups to brainstorm and build on each other's ideas. The business analyst should use this technique to add energy to the group, accommodate large groups, and allow more time for thinking than the typical brainstorming session allows. Using a form or flip chart, groups of five or six people each write three ideas. Then they pass the forms around for other participants to add their ideas. This method generates many ideas in a short time.

+ **Anonymous brainstorming.** In this brainstorming technique, participants anonymously write their ideas on a piece of paper. The papers are tossed into a box and drawn out one by one for the team to discuss. No names or group affiliations are identified to keep anonymity and encourage discovery and discussion by all participants.

+ **Idea mapping.** A facilitator uses this graphical tool to identify affected areas, dependencies, and issues related to the problem being solved. See Figure 4-5 for an example of idea mapping.

+ **20 Questions.** This approach provides the group with a powerful problem-solving strategy. 20 questions is best used when the problem is associated with a single element of a complex system. Referred to as a binary search when it is used to conduct a computerized search, 20 questions is one of the fastest search methods. Lists of items are continually divided in half as yes/no questions are asked. With this tool, a facilita-

Figure 4-5—Idea Mapping

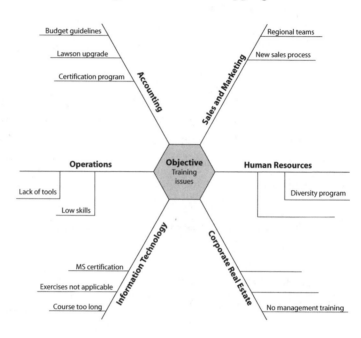

tor challenges assumptions and does not directly focus on the cause of the problem.

The business analyst builds a list of questions asking *if an element of the system can be eliminated as a cause,* and begins to ask the questions. Hopefully, half of the alternatives can be eliminated with each question. When most of the potential causes have been eliminated, the business analyst facilitates a discussion to form a hypothesis about what caused the problem. At this point, the fishbone diagram can be used to determine the possible root causes. See Figure 4-6 for an example of the 20 questions technique.

Figure 4-6—20 Questions

	What?	Where?	When?	Who?	How?
Current State	What happens?	Where is there confusion?	When is it done?	Who does the work?	How are the activities sequenced?
Future State	What should it look like?	Where will the process change?	When will it change?	Who will do the work?	How will the activities be timed and resourced?
Gap Indicators	What is different?	Where will the change make a difference?	When are the differences considered?	Who will identify and validate the gaps?	How will the gaps be improved and managed?
Is There a Better Way?	What alternative solutions are available?	Where would the alternative solution be considered?	When is there a better window of opportunity?	Who makes the decision on an alternative solution?	How will the alternative solution be viewed by the organization?

+ **Sequential Questioning.** Using this technique, the business analyst initiates a discussion or discovery session by proposing a series of questions. Each question is documented on a flip chart page. The initial questions are written at the big-picture level, followed by subsequent questions that progressively elaborate more detail of the topic. By starting with the big view and decomposing the topic into smaller components, the participants address the topic with a thorough and complete approach.

+ **Affinity Diagram.** Affinity diagrams are useful to narrow the discussion because they organize like ideas. They are used when creative or intuitive thinking is required. The sequential questioning technique addresses the issue in a top-down manner, whereas the affinity diagram identifies and organizes ideas from the bottom up, without predetermined restrictions or constraints on the discussion. Groups use this tool to clarify complex issues and reach a consensus on the definition of a problem. It answers a "what" question. For example, it might be used to answer the question "What are the root causes of events that determined or impacted the quality of our product?" Making an affinity diagram can be quite time-consuming, but is a valuable activity. The facilitator involves the entire group in creating an affinity diagram, following these steps:

1. Gather individuals' ideas on sticky notes passed up to the front of the room.

2. Group the notes on the basis of themes.

3. Label the groups.

4. Draw the diagram by placing related notes near each other.

5. Rank categories and combine duplicate issues to create the final, simpler diagram.

Multivoting

Multivoting is a group technique used to prioritize ideas to quickly select the most important or most popular items from a list. It is accomplished through a series of votes, each cutting the list in half. Multivoting often follows a brainstorming session and is used to select the most important items from a list of brainstormed items with limited discussion and difficulty. A list of 30 to 50 items can be reduced to a workable number in 4 or 5 votes. First, count the items and divide by 5 to get the number of possible votes per team member. The facilitator conducts a multivote by following these steps:

1. Generate a list.

2. Combine similar items; an affinity chart might be used to eliminate redundancy.

3. Ask team members to narrow the list by selecting the most important items on the list; allow each participant a number of choices equal to one-fifth of the total number of items.

4. Tally the votes by asking each participant to put a checkmark by his or her choices.

5. Eliminate those with few or no votes.

6. Repeat steps 3 through 5.

7. The items that remain are candidates for further analysis by the group.

Nominal Group Technique

Nominal group technique (NGT) is a more structured approach than brainstorming or multivoting, but it is similar to both. NGT is a consensus planning technique that helps prioritize ideas. It is referred to as "nominal" because the group doesn't engage in the usual amount of interaction. It is useful when all or some of the group members are new to the team or when the group is quite large. It is an extremely effective technique for highly controversial issues or when the team seems to be stuck in disagreement. The facilitator conducts an NGT session by following these steps:

◆ Part One: Individual Brainstorm

1. The facilitator defines the issue or problem and describes the purpose of the session and the procedures.

2. After discussion to clarify the issue and the process, each participant is asked to generate and document ideas.

3. The facilitator then goes around the room and asks each participant to present one idea. The idea is captured on a flipchart. After the first round, participants are asked for a second and third response, until all ideas have been captured.

4. The facilitator then leads a discussion to clarify and discuss ideas and condenses the list by combining like ideas.

◆ **Part Two: Making the Selection**

1. Reduce the list by multivoting (see above).

2. The facilitator asks each participant to individually make selections by writing one item on a card. Limit the number of cards to four to six for each member.

3. Ask participants to assign points based on the number of index cards (for four cards, assign the number 4 to the most preferred item).

4. Tally votes and discuss results.

Decision Grids

Decision grids are useful when facilitating a group to examine all possible alternatives that were identified during the brainstorming session prior to making the decision. A sample decision grid appears in Table 4-7. The process for using the grid is as follows:

1. Define the problem or issue clearly; note on a flip chart.

2. Brainstorm potential options to resolve the problem or issue (see brainstorming techniques earlier in this chapter).

3. Describe each option in enough detail so that all participants understand the option.

4. Facilitate a discussion to complete the information desired about each option. (Be sure to define the criteria to ensure that all participants understand the categories.)

5. Step back and ask the group which options appear to be the best in terms of lowest time, cost, and risk and highest value to the business.

Table 4-7—Decision Grid

Option	Cost	Time	Risk	Impact	Effort	Pros	Cons	Business Value
A								
B								
C								
D								
E								

Group Focus—Keeping Meetings on Track

A good facilitator provides the structure and process needed for the participants to work together effectively. The facilitator notices, through verbal and nonverbal cues, when participants are disturbed or bored and have mentally checked out of the meeting. Through experience, the business analyst learns effective meeting facilitation techniques and knows when to intervene, summarize, and move the group on and when to let the discussion continue.

In addition to the facilitation techniques discussed in this chapter, several meeting management techniques are essential to keeping the meeting on track, including those listed in Table 4-8.

Table 4-8—Meeting Management Techniques

Technique	Description
Plan	• Successful meeting execution depends heavily on adequate meeting planning
Use the agenda	• Understand and use the power of the agenda—your tool to manage the meeting and keep it on track
Start and end on time	• Always start the meeting on time, even if key participants have not yet arrived; if necessary, rearrange agenda items until required participants are present
Facilitate	Keep in mind your role as meeting facilitator. Your responsibilities are to: • Open the meeting • Use a short warm-up activity to get the group focused • Review or reference the meeting ground rules that have been established by the team members and secure participants' agreement to assist in keeping to the ground rules • Review the agenda and secure participants' agreement to assist in keeping to the agenda • Make sure someone is recording the meeting minutes and helping you keep track of time • Move through the agenda one item at a time
Keep the discussions focused	• Table items that are not on the agenda for future meetings; capture items in a parking lot to be considered in the future so that the owner of the item can let it go and redirect attention to the agenda item
Keep timing appropriate	• Establish an appropriate pace; do not rush to decisions; remain patient
Lead discussions	• Facilitate discussions by setting up the topic, soliciting comments and opinions, reframing and summarizing, closing the discussion, and moving on to the next agenda item
Manage behaviors	• Encourage full participation by drawing in those that are not involved and encouraging positive comments
Close the meeting	• Capture action items or next steps • Set agenda for the next meeting • Set date, time, and place for next meeting • Evaluate the meeting effectiveness • Congratulate the group on its progress

We will now turn our attention to specific meetings that the business analyst leads during the life of the project. It might appear that we are focusing our attention primarily on the meetings the business analyst conducts during the requirements phase. However, the requirements elicitation, analysis, specification, documentation, and validation activities are not linear; they are very much iterative and occur throughout the project.

For each meeting we provide a description of the meeting, its benefits, its challenges, the participants, the strategy for conducting the meeting, inputs to the meeting, outputs or results of the meeting, and a proposed facilitator agenda. A facilitator agenda differs from a standard meeting agenda in that it provides facilitation suggestions, tools, and techniques to lead the group through each agenda item.

Endnotes

1. Brad Spangler. "Facilitation," *Beyond Intractability*, 2003. Online at www.beyondintractability.org/essay/facilitation/ (accessed August 10, 2007).

2. Miranda Duncan. *Effective Meeting Facilitation: The Sine Qua Non of Planning*. Online at http://arts.endow.gov/resources/Lessons?DUNCAN1.html (accessed October 17, 2006).

3. Fran Rees. *How to Lead Work Teams: Facilitation Skills*, 2001. San Francisco: Jossey-Bass/Pfeiffer.

4. Peter R. Scholtes, Brian L. Joiner, and Barbara J. Streibel. *The Team Handbook*, 3rd ed., 2003. Madison, WI: Oriel, Inc.

5. Ibid.

6. Miranda Duncan. *Effective Meeting Facilitation: The Sine Qua Non of Planning*. Online at http://arts.endow.gov/resources/Lessons?DUNCAN1.html (accessed October 17, 2006).

7.   Fran Rees. *How to Lead Work Teams: Facilitation Skills*, 2001. San Francisco: Jossey-Bass/Pfeiffer.

8.   David C. Kolb. *Team Leadership*, 1996. Durago, CO: Lore International Institute.

Chapter 5

Requirements Elicitation Meetings

In This Chapter:

- Challenges
- Roles and Responsibilities
- Individual and Small Group Interviews
- Facilitated Requirements Elicitation Workshops

Requirements elicitation involves conducting initial requirements-gathering sessions with customers, users, and stakeholders to begin the documentation process. Requirements-gathering techniques include discovery sessions, facilitated workshops, interviews, surveys, prototyping, review of existing system and business documents, and note-taking and feedback loops to customers, users, and stakeholders.

The purposes of requirements elicitation are to:

+ Identify the customers, users, and stakeholders to determine who should be involved in the requirements-gathering process

+ Understand the business goals and objectives and identify the essential user tasks that support the organizational goals

+ Identify and define requirements to understand the needs of the users, customers, and stakeholders

The first iterations of the business requirements document and the requirements management plan are the key outputs of this activity. A well-planned and executed set of requirements elicitation activities forms the foundation for requirements analysis, specification, documentation, and validation.

Challenges

Several challenges are associated with requirements elicitation, including:

+ Securing adequate time and the appropriate resources for elicitation activities

+ Building requirements from the top down so that the requirements team understands the big picture

Roles and Responsibilities

The following roles and responsibilities apply to requirements elicitation activities:

+ **Project sponsor.** Authorizes and funds the requirements elicitation activities.

+ **Facilitator.** Designs, plans, and leads the elicitation sessions using effective facilitation and business analysis skills, tools, and techniques.

+ **Business analyst.** The business analyst is a core project team member who leads stakeholder representatives to elicit, analyze, specify, validate, and manage project requirements throughout the life cycle.

+ **Project team.** Contribute to the discovery of requirements and begin building relationships with key stakeholders.

+ **Requirements team.** Support the elicitation, analysis, documentation, specification, and validation of requirements.

+ **Business users and subject matter experts.** Contribute to the discovery of requirements needed to solve the business problem and seize the new business opportunity.

+ **Scribe.** Captures and documents the work results of elicitation sessions. The person in this role is often skilled in requirements analysis and modeling tools.

The requirements elicitation meetings discussed in detail in this chapter include:

+ Individual and small group interviews

+ Facilitated requirements elicitation workshops

Individual and Small Group Interviews

Interviews are conducted with members of management and subject matter experts of the business area undergoing change, and with members of the performing organization that will develop the solution. The objectives of the interviews are to gain an initial understanding of the scope of the project and to capture any management-level assumptions and constraints. In addition, the business analyst presents the requirements activities and plans, and secures approval to use resources in the requirements activities.

Once approval is secured to begin the requirements elicitation process, the business analyst conducts small-group or one-on-one interviews to begin to draft high-level requirements documentation. This might include documenting the scope of requirements, preparing a high-level context diagram (also referred to as a super system model), or identifying functional requirements categories (sometimes documented as use case names). The business analyst begins to draft the glossary of terms as well.

Purpose and Benefits

Interviewing management and small groups of experts helps to:

- Obtain management approval to invite people to participate in requirements elicitation, analysis, specification, and validation activities

- Build draft documentation to be used as a starting point when conducting formal workshops and review sessions

Challenges

Key challenges include:

- Getting time on the calendars of the functional managers that own the resources

- Making the business case and securing management approval for dedicated resources for the full scope of requirements activities

- Identifying all relevant project stakeholders

Who Should Attend?

Typically, some or all of the core project team—consisting of the business analyst, the business representative, the technical lead, and the project manager—attend initial requirements elicitation interviews.

Meeting Strategy

The business analyst and project manager meet with their immediate supervisors to identify key management and subject matter experts and secure approval to schedule time on their calendars. Management interview preparation and execution steps include:

1. **Prepare for the interview**

   - Carefully review the business case and project charter documents. Identify any questions, gaps, or ambiguities that need clarification.

   - Determine the composition of the interview team. The interview team should include at least two people but no more than three.

   - Define the interview team roles. The roles include questioner (there should be one main questioner), note taker, observer, and timekeeper.

   - Determine the interview strategy, including key areas to discuss, specific questions for individuals, time to spend on each area or question, specific documents to review or discuss.

   - Prepare the interview agenda, capturing each area of discussion.

2. **Conduct the interview**

   - Begin the interview by putting the interviewee at ease. It is usually desirable to conduct the interview in a private office. Emphasize the confidentiality of the information. No comment will be attributed to any one person. Introduce the interview team. Ask the interviewee to introduce himself or herself and to brief you on his or her role in the project.

+ The business analyst or project manager typically leads the discussion. Anyone on the interview team may ask follow-up questions. Probe for and discuss management expectations, business problems or needs, understanding of the project scope, time, cost, and other constraints. Determine the manager's understanding of the priority among the elements of the triple constraint—time, cost, and scope/quality. End the interview by asking open-ended questions.

3. Debrief

+ Immediately after the interview, the business analyst facilitates a discussion with the interview team to arrive at consensus on the information gleaned from the interview. The note taker integrates comments from the debriefing session into the notes.

+ The note taker documents the results of the interview in the form of an interview report; presents the report to the interview team for their comments, recommendations, and refinement; and updates the report with the feedback.

+ The business analyst incorporates the information in the interview report into the business requirements document or the requirements management plan.

Inputs

+ Business case

+ Project charter

Outputs

+ Stakeholder list and analysis of stakeholders' influence and expertise

+ Interview notes

+ Draft business requirements document, requirements management plan, and context diagram prepared from information gleaned during the interviews

Facilitator Agenda

The agenda for interviews must be customized for each person or group to be interviewed. Design your agenda to maximize information discovery and support. A sample agenda is shown in Figure 5-1.

Figure 5-1—Management Interview Facilitator Agenda

General Information	
Date:	Time:
Subject:	Location:
Meeting Sponsor:	Facilitator:
Project Manager:	Business Analyst:
Project Name:	Project ID:
Meeting Objectives:	Conduct initial interviews with management to fully understand the business needs and expectations of management

Attendees					
Attended	Name	Business Area Representing	Attended	Name	Business Area Representing

Figure 5-1—Management Interview Facilitator Agenda, continued

Agenda Topic	Pre-senter	Allotted Time	Facilitator Agenda	Facilitation Tools and Techniques
1. Introductions and overview of interview process	Facilitator		Set the tone of the interview. Foster an honest and positive environment to ensure a productive meeting. Emphasize the confidentiality of the interview and all discussions. • Open interview with an ice breaker or introductions if required. • Review meeting purpose and objectives. • Review interview agenda and timeline. **Facilitator should ask:** • Are there any other expectations for this interview?	• Interview process document • Ice breaker activity • Interview agenda
2. Review interview ground rules	Facilitator		Develop a straw man of interview ground rules prior to meeting. • Review the interview ground rules for understanding and commitment. **Facilitator should ask:** • Are there any changes or additions to the rules?	• Interview ground rules document • Ground rules can be sent out in advance with the agenda

Figure 5-1—Management Interview Facilitator Agenda, continued

Agenda Topic	Pre-senter	Allotted Time	Facilitator Agenda	Facilitation Tools and Techniques
3. Business need	Facilita-tor and interview team		Ensure that the interviewees understand the business need. **Facilitator should ask:** • What elements of the business need require more clarification? • How is the proposed change aligned with the organizational strategy and the business initiatives? • Will this project address the organizational issues? • What happens if we do nothing? • Is the proposed solution addressing the true problem?	• A straw man or the approved business case • A straw man or the approved project charter • Discussion techniques • Questioning techniques • Work the questions from a macro level to a micro level to ensure a clear view of the answer and 　• Obtain more detail 　• Understand impacts 　• Discover symptoms

Figure 5-1—Management Interview Facilitator Agenda, continued

Agenda Topic	Pre-senter	Allotted Time	Facilitator Agenda	Facilitation Tools and Techniques
4. Project goals and objectives	Facilitator and interview team		**Project Goal** A project goal provides a common understanding of *what* is to be accomplished and *why* it is needed. This forms the foundation for what is to be measured. • To (action verb such as "provide" or "produce") (service or product) to (customer) in order to (why the service or product is needed). **Facilitator should ask:** • Do you agree with the goal statement? If not, what would you change? **Project Objectives** The project objectives describe the strategy of how the organization will achieve the goal. • To (action verb such as "improve" or "reduce") (what is to accomplished) by (a number, metric, date). **Facilitator should ask:** • Do you agree with the objectives? If not, what would you change?	• Goal/objective statement template • Questioning techniques • Draft of levels 1 and 2 of work breakdown structure
5. Project scope	Facilitator and interview team		Review what is in scope and out of scope for each project objective. **Facilitator should ask:** • Do you agree with the identified scope and why? • Are there any additional scope items to consider? • What is the organization willing to take on to complete this objective? • What is the organization not willing to take on to complete this objective?	• A straw man or the approved business case • A straw man or the approved project charter • Discussion techniques • Questioning techniques • Draft of work breakdown structure

Figure 5-1—Management Interview Facilitator Agenda, continued

Agenda Topic	Pre-senter	Allotted Time	Facilitator Agenda	Facilitation Tools and Techniques
6. Measures of success	Facilitator and interview team		To measure success, you first need to define what success will be. It needs to be measured by: • What is project performance success? • What is product, service, or solution success? **Facilitator should ask:** • What indicators will measure success? • What would success look like? • How will we know we have successfully delivered the solution?	• Discussion techniques • Questioning techniques • Draft of work break-down structure
7. Stakeholders	Facilitator and interview team		Review the current list of primary and secondary stakeholders. **Facilitator should ask:** • Is there anyone on this list who is not affected by this project? • What other stakeholders need to be added to the list? • Do any of these persons disagree with this solution and how would they argue their case? • Are there political considerations with any of these persons that need to be addressed? • What sources of resistance will we need to address? • Who from this list are the project champions? • Who are the players that need to be involved? • How will this stakeholder affect the results? • What are the strengths and/or weaknesses of this stakeholder? • What will it take to get buy-in from this stakeholder? • What role would this stakeholder play?	• Stakeholder list • Stakeholder analysis tools • Stakeholder influence matrix • Stakeholder impact table • Communications plan

Figure 5-1—Management Interview Facilitator Agenda, continued

Agenda Topic	Pre-senter	Allotted Time	Facilitator Agenda	Facilitation Tools and Techniques
8. Summarize interview	Facilitator and interview team		Provide a brief summary of items discussed. **Facilitator should ask:** • Just to summarize, we discussed the following . . . • What we heard you say is . . . • Have we understood this correctly? • Are there any additional questions or concerns? • Is there anything else you would like to add?	
9. Overview of requirements process	Facilitator		• Provide an overview of the requirements process. • Discuss timelines for requirement deliverables. • Discuss needed resources for the requirements process and obtain approval for resources and/or commitment to participate by the interviewee. **Facilitator should ask:** • What are your expectations of the requirements process? • What issues have you encountered in the past with requirements? • How can the requirements process be improved? • How committed are you to the requirements process?	Requirements process document

Figure 5-1—Management Interview Facilitator Agenda, continued

Agenda Topic	Pre-senter	Allotted Time	Facilitator Agenda	Facilitation Tools and Techniques
10. Review next steps	Facilitator		Facilitator should ask: • Are there any questions? • Do we have your approval to proceed with requirements elicitation and analysis?	• Parking board templates • Issues log • Action item log • Risk log • Constraints log • Parking lot • Project repository guidelines
11. Close interview	Facilitator		Thank the interviewee for his or her time and contribution.	

Facilitated Requirements Elicitation Workshops

The requirements elicitation workshop is perhaps the most important event planned and facilitated by the business analyst. According to Ellen Gottesdiener, a requirements workshop is a structured meeting in which a carefully selected group of stakeholders and content experts work together to define, create, refine, and reach closure on deliverables such as models and documents that represent user requirements.[1] The requirements workshop is similar to the joint application design (JAD) workshop developed by IBM in the late 1970s to help groups to build high-quality requirements and design deliverables.

Purpose and Benefits

Using structured workshops to progressively elaborate requirements can:

+ Bring together project stakeholders, including customers, users, and developers

+ Encourage team communication, decision-making, and a common understanding of the business area undergoing change and the nature of the change

+ Validate the scope of work

+ Define business requirements collaboratively

+ Reach an agreement or consensus on the recommended solution

Challenges

Challenges encountered when planning and conducting requirements workshops include:

- Determining whether requirements workshops are appropriate for the project (workshops are not recommended for small, low-risk projects)

- Planning sufficiently, including the number of workshops and deliverables produced at each workshop

- Selecting effective workshop facilitation and requirements documentation techniques

- Ensuring that the right participants are present and actively involved in each workshop

- Managing participant behaviors and hidden agendas

- Managing time throughout the workshop to ensure that desired deliverables are produced

Who Should Attend?

Requirements elicitation meetings are planned and facilitated by the business analyst and assisted by a scribe who is proficient in capturing information in real time. These are usually relatively large workshops with key business and technical subject matter experts in attendance, including:

- Project sponsor to kick off the workshop

- Requirements team members

- Core project team members (project manager, business analyst, technical lead, business visionary)

- Key sources for requirements such as internal and external business users and business and technical subject matter experts

Meeting Strategy

Typically the project manager conducts a project kickoff workshop to formally launch the project and define the project charter, scope, objectives, assumptions, and constraints. The business analyst then plans and facilitates requirements elicitation workshops in a top-down manner to progressively elaborate the requirements. It is recommended that the business analyst:

+ Spend considerable time planning for the workshop with the core project team members.

+ Design a sequence of activities to progressively elaborate requirements, deliver the selected requirements artifacts, and foster mutual learning, understanding, consensus, and teamwork.

+ Kick off the meeting, set expectations, and establish a collaborative atmosphere.

+ Begin with a project overview and set scope boundaries (for the first workshop, perhaps the project manager or project sponsor also presents broad project information).

+ Ensure full participation by helping participants build relationships; taking advantage of the expertise, styles. and contributions of each person; and building a high-performing team.

+ If using use cases to define requirements, the business analyst would likely conduct three tiers of workshops. At the workshop, an effective approach is to divide the participants into break-out groups of five to nine people to develop:

  □ Tier 1 Workshop—the scope of requirements in terms of context diagram, use case names, and a glossary of terms

□ Tier 2 Workshop—the high-level requirements in terms of a description of use cases, business rules, and scenarios

□ Tier 3 Workshop—the detailed requirements in terms of detailed scenarios, domain models, and prototype screens

+ The break-out groups then report back to the full requirements team, and the business analyst facilitates a discussion to elicit comments, suggestions, and refinement. The facilitator works with the group to ensure that the content is at the right level of detail and degree of quality, and that consensus is achieved.

Inputs

+ Business case

+ Project charter

+ Interview notes

+ Draft business requirements document, requirements management plan, and context diagram prepared from information gleaned during the interviews

Outputs

+ Draft business requirements documents and artifacts

+ Updated stakeholder analysis

+ Documented issues, risks, assumptions, constraints, and action items

+ Schedule of remaining requirements activities

Facilitator Agenda

The agenda for a requirements elicitation workshop must be customized for each project. Design your agenda to maximize information discovery, creation, and elaboration. A sample agenda for an elicitation session using the case approach is shown in Figure 5-2.

Figure 5-2—Requirements Elicitation Workshop Facilitator Agenda

General Information	
Date:	Time:
Subject:	Location:
Meeting Sponsor:	Facilitator:
Project Manager:	Business Analyst:
Project Name:	Project ID:
Workshop Objectives:	◆ Supports a collaborative approach to requirements elicitation ◆ Facilitates techniques to enable teams to focus on effective requirement identification ◆ Builds a foundation for successful requirements analysis ◆ Reinforces complete and thorough identification of affected stakeholders

Attendees					
Attended	Name	Business Area Representing	Attended	Name	Business Area Representing

Figure 5-2—Requirements Elicitation Workshop Facilitator Agenda, continued

Topic	Presenter	Allotted Time	Facilitator Agenda	Facilitation Tools and Techniques
1. Open workshop	Project sponsor		Project sponsor opens the workshop. The sponsor should set the tone to foster an honest and positive environment. The project sponsor will: • Provide an overview of the business need • Review meeting goals and objectives • Communicate workshop measures of success **Project Goal** A project goal provides a common understanding of what is to be accomplished and *why* it is needed. This forms the foundation for what is to be measured. • To (action verb such as "provide" or "produce") (service or product) to (customer) in order to (why the service or product is needed). **Project Objectives** The project objectives describe the strategy of how the organization will achieve the goal. • To (action verb such as "improve" or "reduce") (what is to be accomplished) by (a number, metric, date).	• Meet with project sponsor in advance to review the role he or she will play during the workshop • Communicate the workshop goals and approach • Goal/objective statement template • Questioning techniques • Draft of levels 1 and 2 of work breakdown structure

Figure 5-2—Requirements Elicitation Workshop Facilitator Agenda, continued

Topic	Presenter	Allotted Time	Facilitator Agenda	Facilitation Tools and Techniques
2. Workshop overview, introductions and expectations	Facilitator		Conduct an ice breaker activity to: • Introduce participants to each other • Begin to foster team collaboration • Review the workshop agenda and timeline Conduct a round robin exercise to identify participants. It is important for participants to clearly understand the purpose and work to be completed during the workshop. If expectations are not aligned, work toward clarification to ensure workshop success. **Facilitator should ask:** • What expectations do you have for this workshop? • Are there any other expectations for this workshop? Begin managing participants' expectations for the work to be completed. Document the participants' expectations on a flip chart page and post the page on the wall. These expectations will be reviewed at the close of the workshop to ensure that all expectations were met.	• Ice breaker activity • Workshop agenda • Round robin technique to explore workshop expectations • Flip chart to capture workshop expectations

Figure 5-2—Requirements Elicitation Workshop Facilitator Agenda, continued

Topic	Presenter	Allotted Time	Facilitator Agenda	Facilitation Tools and Techniques
3. Workshop ground rules	Facilitator		Develop a set of team and decision-making ground rules prior to the workshop. Send the ground rules with the agenda in advance. Review the ground rules with participants at the beginning of the workshop. **Facilitator should ask:** ♦ Does everyone agree with the rules? ♦ Are there any changes or additions to the rules? ♦ Will these rules foster a collaborative and team working environment? ♦ Are there any off-limits topics? ♦ As a team, how should we handle any hidden agendas?	♦ Ground rules template ♦ Questioning sequence techniques ♦ Multivote technique for approval

Figure 5-2—Requirements Elicitation Workshop Facilitator Agenda, continued

Topic	Presenter	Allotted Time	Facilitator Agenda	Facilitation Tools and Techniques
4. Overview of parking boards	Facilitator		Prepare parking boards in advance. Use a flip chart for each parking board and position it so that it is visible to all participants and easy for the facilitator to access. A parking lot is a component of the parking boards. Parking boards are flip charts marked with titles that represent categories of information. They are used to capture the information during facilitated sessions in real time. A flip chart page for each type of parking board is placed on the wall to begin capturing items in the following categories: • Parking lot • Assumptions • Risks • Constraints • Issues • Action Items Review the purpose of parking boards with workshop attendees. **Parking lot:** a tool to track questions that require follow-up. **Issue:** a concern raised by any stakeholder that requires a decision or resolution. **Action items:** a list of follow-up actions that are assigned an owner and a timeframe for completion. **Risk:** an uncertain event or condition that, if it occurs, has a positive or negative effect on a project's objectives. **Constraint:** a restriction or limitation with which the team must comply throughout the project. **Facilitator should ask:** Are there any questions about the parking boards?	• Flip chart techniques • Parking board definitions

Figure 5-2—Requirements Elicitation Workshop Facilitator Agenda, continued

Topic	Presenter	Allotted Time	Facilitator Agenda	Facilitation Tools and Techniques
5. Overview of housekeeping items	Facilitator		Review housekeeping items and ensure that participants understand each housekeeping item. • Facilities orientation • Breaks and lunch • Emergencies • Minimizing interruptions	

6. Review business need	Facilitator		It is important to ensure that there is consensus on the business case. If not, identify and work to resolve any issues before proceeding with the remainder of the workshop.
			Facilitator should ask:
			• What elements of the business need require more clarification?
			• How is the proposed change aligned with the organizational strategy and the business initiatives?
			• Will this project address the organizational issues?
			• What would happen if we do nothing?
			• Is the proposed solution addressing the true problem?
			• Are there any questions, concerns, issues, or constraints with the identified business need?
				• A straw man or the approved business case
				• A straw man or the approved project charter
				• Discussion techniques
				• Questioning techniques
				• Work the questions from a macro level to a micro level to ensure a clear view of the answer and:
				  • Obtain more detail
				  • Understand impacts
				  • Discover symptoms

Figure 5-2—Requirements Elicitation Workshop Facilitator Agenda, continued

Topic	Presenter	Allotted Time	Facilitator Agenda	Facilitation Tools and Techniques
7. Validate the behavior of the affected system and verify scope	Participants		Prepare a straw man context diagram to validate and reach consensus on the system behavior. **Facilitator should ask:** • What actions happen within the system? • When will these actions occur? • What will the system do automatically? • What manual activities must be performed? Once the context diagram is completed, validate and/or align the system behavior with the scope of the project. **Facilitator should ask:** • Have all scope items been identified? If not, what scope should be added? • Have all the out-of-scope items been identified? If not, what out-of-scope items should be documented?	• Context diagram • Event tables • Event lists • Parking boards • Brainstorming techniques • Questioning techniques
8. Business policies	Participants		Policies affect how the system will be implemented and how the manual process will be worked. They are constraints that must be identified and managed by the team throughout the requirements process. Once identified, group and allocate the policies into the system domains. Validate the policies that are within the scope of the project. **Facilitator should ask:** • What policies must be enforced for each business process? • What standards and regulations govern the business? • What policies support the business goals?	• List of external regulations, standards, and legislative documents • List of internal business rules • Parking boards • Brainstorming techniques • Questioning techniques • Consensus techniques

Figure 5-2—Requirements Elicitation Workshop Facilitator Agenda, continued

Topic	Presenter	Allotted Time	Facilitator Agenda	Facilitation Tools and Techniques
9. Develop actor tables	Participants		Explain to workshop participants the purpose of the actor table. The purpose is to identify and categorize all affected system users. Understanding the roles and responsibilities within the system ensures that all stakeholders and interactions within the system are analyzed for complete and accurate requirements. **Facilitator should ask:** • Who needs to interact with the system? • What is their primary role? • What responsibilities are included as the actor interacts with the system?	• User roles • Actor table template • Straw man actor map • Parking boards • Brainstorming techniques • Questioning techniques • Consensus techniques
10. Develop lists of use cases	Participants		A use case is a text or graphical description of how the actors use the system to accomplish the goals. Each use case is an identified functionality within the system. Work as a team to identify all related functions within the system. **Facilitator should ask:** • What are the goals for each actor within the system? • What steps must happen within each event? • Are there multiple events within each goal?	• Straw man use case diagram • Brainstorming techniques • Questioning techniques • Consensus techniques • Parking boards

Figure 5-2—Requirements Elicitation Workshop Facilitator Agenda, continued

Topic	Presenter	Allotted Time	Facilitator Agenda	Facilitation Tools and Techniques
11. Document a brief description for each use case	Participants		Begin documenting a brief description of each use case. Include the following: • Use case category • Use case name • Brief explanation • Initiating actor • Secondary actor • Triggering events • Inputs • Outputs • Exceptions • Business rules	• Use case log • Use case template • Brainstorming techniques • Questioning techniques • Consensus techniques • Parking boards
12. Document each use case	Participants		Work in team or subteams to identify the activities and/or steps that must happen to accomplish the use case goal. **Facilitator should ask:** • What activities must happen for the actor to complete the goal? • Has the team verified that the steps are in the correct order? • Were any steps missed? • Are there any variations or exceptions to this event? • What are the steps for the exception? • Has the team identified any subevents with this use case? • Have all business rules been identified? • Have any issues, constraints, or risks been identified?	• Use case diagram • Use case map • Use case packages • Use case matrix • Brainstorming techniques • Questioning techniques • Consensus techniques • Parking boards

Figure 5-2—Requirements Elicitation Workshop Facilitator Agenda, continued

Topic	Presenter	Allotted Time	Facilitator Agenda	Facilitation Tools and Techniques
13. Review use cases	Participants		Post the completed work on the wall or overhead projector. Review the work completed by the team and subteams for any corrections and/or modifications needed. In some instances this might require an additional meeting or workshop after the participants have had an opportunity to review all the work completed. **Facilitator should ask:** • Is any additional detail required? • Are there any modifications? • Have all issues, risks, and constraints been identified?	• Questioning techniques • Consensus techniques • Parking boards

Figure 5-2—Requirements Elicitation Workshop Facilitator Agenda, continued

Topic	Presenter	Allotted Time	Facilitator Agenda	Facilitation Tools and Techniques

14. Review parking boards and next steps	Facilitator		• Review the parking boards.
			• Assign a due date and owner to each action item or issue for resolution.
			• Categorize the risks and document them in the risk log.
			• Review next steps and associated timelines. This should include:
			  • Issue resolution
			  • Action items
			  • Distribution of workshop results
			• Communicate when and where the workshop results will be published for review and required follow-up.
			• Inform the interviewee of the project repository location.
			Facilitator should ask:
			• Are there any questions?
			• Are there any corrections to the parking board items?
			• Does the team have your commitment to complete the assigned next steps?
				• Parking board templates
				• Issues log
				• Action item log
				• Risk log
				• Constraints log
				• Parking lot
				• Project repository guidelines

15. Evaluate and close workshop	Facilitator		• Review the workshop goals and objectives. • Conduct a workshop evaluation to validate whether the measures of success have been met. • Conduct a lessons learned discussion to identify ways to improve workshop performance. • Thank participants for their time and contributions.	• Workshop agenda with goals, objectives, and measures of success • Workshop evaluation form • Lessons learned template

Endnote

1.   Ellen Gottesdiener. *Requirements by Collaboration: Workshops for Defining Needs*, 2002. Boston: Pearson Education, Addison-Wesley Professional.

Chapter 6

Requirements Analysis Meetings

In This Chapter:

- Challenges
- Business Modeling Workshops
- Types of Analysis Meetings
- Business Process Modeling Workshops
- Prototype Review Meetings
- Risk Management Workshops

Requirements are first stated in simple terms and are then analyzed and decomposed for clarity. *Requirements analysis* is the process of grouping requirements information into various categories, evaluating requirements for selected qualities, representing requirements in different forms, deriving detailed requirements from high-level requirements, and negotiating priorities. Requirements analysis also includes activities to determine required function and performance characteristics, the context of implementation, stakeholder constraints and measures of effectiveness, and validation criteria. Through the analysis process, requirements are decomposed and captured in a combination of text and graphical formats.

The purpose of analysis activities is to restate requirements in different forms to clarify and further define the nature and scope of the requirement. In addition, the feasibility of the requirements is analyzed and the risks are assessed.

Requirements analysis activities remove requirements gaps and ambiguities. Through analysis, requirements information is progressively elaborated to ensure completeness and accuracy.

Challenges

Over the past few decades, a bewildering array of business analysis techniques have been developed to describe business processes, policies, and systems. It is difficult for the business analyst to determine which techniques to use. In practice, just a few models and diagrams are used to provide a complete picture of the business need. Please refer to *Getting it Right: Business Requirement Analysis Tools and Techniques* for a discussion of the recommended business analysis models. Most analysis workshops involve modeling the business.

Business Modeling Workshops

Business modeling sessions restate requirements in the form of diagrams and structured text. Models include both text and drawings. A requirements model is a blueprint for a process, information flows, or solution components that can take the form of a diagram, list, or table, supplemented with descriptive text that depicts a business need from a particular point of view.

Purpose and Benefits

Requirements models facilitate communication and understanding among business and technical stakeholders. Through the process of creating the models, missing and incomplete requirements are often discovered.

Challenges

The biggest obstacle in business requirements modeling is knowing which models to create. When selecting the appropriate models, the business analyst must understand their basic purposes and what they are intended to communicate. Again, refer to *Getting it Right: Business Requirements Analysis Tools and Techniques* for a discussion of the recommended business analysis models.

Who Should Attend?

The business analyst plans and facilitates requirements analysis meetings. These meetings are usually small working sessions with key subject matter experts in the room, assisted by a scribe who is proficient in capturing models and diagrams in real time.

Meeting Strategy

The business analyst plans and facilitates the analysis meeting to complete the following activities:

- Modeling requirements to restate and clarify them. Modeling is accomplished at the appropriate usage, process, or detailed structural level.

- Studying requirements feasibility to determine whether the requirement is viable technically, operationally, and economically; trading off requirements to determine the most feasible requirement alternatives.

- Assessing requirement risks and constraints and modifying requirements to mitigate identified risks. The goal is to reduce requirement risks through early validation prototyping techniques.

- Deriving additional requirements as more is learned about the business need.

Inputs

- Business case

- Project charter

- Interview notes

- Draft business requirements document, requirements management plan, and other diagrams prepared from information gleaned during the interviews and workshops

- Stakeholder analysis

- Documented issues, risks, constraints, and action items

- Schedule of remaining requirements activities

Outputs

Examples of requirement models include:

- Updates to business requirements document and requirements management plan

- New and/or updated requirements understanding diagrams and models

- In/out of scope lists

- Event lists

- Business process flows

- Use cases

- Data models

- Class models

+ Business rules

+ Actor maps

+ Prototypes

+ Interface diagrams

+ Application flows

Types of Analysis Meetings

The requirements analysis meetings discussed in detail in this chapter include:

+ Business process modeling workshop

+ Prototype review meeting

+ Risk workshop

Business Process Modeling Workshops

The business process modeling workshop, shown in Figure 6-1, is a facilitated set of activities designed to guide stakeholders to define or make necessary changes to increase the efficiencies or effectiveness of a business process.

Purpose and Benefits

+ Supports a clear process definition using industry best practices

+ Bridges business areas, information technology, and external and internal stakeholders

+ Improves efficiencies in business performance

+ Supports project risk management

+ Provides a framework for discovery of areas that need improvement

+ Supports resource planning and allocations

+ Enhances effective communications

+ Supports a consistent approach to work

Challenges

+ Securing sufficient time and budget for advanced preparation and planning and workshop sessions

+ Ensuring skilled facilitation

+ Ensuring that the right stakeholders participate

+ Building consensus on the process

Who Should Attend?

+ Project team

+ Key project stakeholders

+ Project sponsor

+ Business users and subject matter experts

Meeting Strategy

+ Define the purpose and objectives of the workshop.

+ Select the right process and subprocesses to map.

+ Meet with the key stakeholders to build a preliminary model.

+ Send an "as is" process model to workshop participants in advance to prepare for workshop activities.

Roles and Responsibilities

+ **Project sponsor:** authorizes and funds the workshop

+ **Facilitator:** designs, plans, and leads the workshop process using effective facilitation skills, tools, and techniques

+ **Project team:** works with stakeholders to define and model the process

+ **Business users and subject matter experts:** contribute to the business model being defined and modeled

+ **Scribe:** captures and documents the work and results of the workshop

Inputs

+ Current "as is" process

+ Process vision and objectives

+ Current process documentation

+ Process modeling methods, standards, and tools

+ List of affected stakeholders

Outputs

- New or improved business process
- Root cause analysis
- Updated stakeholder list
- Prioritized list of improvements to the process

Facilitator Agenda

A sample facilitator agenda for a business modeling workshop is shown in Figure 6-1.

Figure 6-1—Business Modeling Workshop Facilitator Agenda

General Information	
Date:	Time:
Subject:	Location:
Meeting Sponsor:	Facilitator:
Project Manager:	Business Analyst:
Project Name:	Project ID:
Interview Objectives:	• Identify and document "as is" and "future state" processes • Build consensus on future state processes • Identify areas of improvement and/or software requirements to resolve the business need

Attendees		
Attended	Name	Business Area Representing

Figure 6-1—Business Modeling Workshop Facilitator Agenda, continued

Topic	Presenter	Allotted Time	Facilitator Agenda	Facilitation Tools and Techniques
1. Open the process modeling workshop	Project sponsor or key stakeholder		Project sponsor or key stakeholder opens the workshop. He or she should set the tone of the workshop. It is important to foster an honest and positive environment to ensure a productive meeting. Open the meeting by: • Providing an overview of the business need • Reviewing workshop goals and objectives • Communicating workshop measures of success **Facilitator should ask:** • What elements of the business need require more clarification? • Are there any questions, concerns, issues, or constraints regarding the identified business need?	• Meet with project sponsor or key stakeholder in advance to review the role he or she will play during the workshop • Business case or project charter • Questioning techniques

Figure 6-1—Business Modeling Workshop Facilitator Agenda, continued

Topic	Presenter	Allotted Time	Facilitator Agenda	Facilitation Tools and Techniques

2. Workshop overview, introductions, and expectations	Facilitator and process team		• Conduct an ice breaker activity to:
			  • Introduce participants to each other
			  • Begin to foster team collaboration
			• Review workshop agenda and timeline
			• Review workshop roles and responsibilities
			• Conduct a round robin exercise to identify participants' expectations. It is important for participants to clearly understand the purpose and work to be completed during the workshop. If expectations are not aligned, work toward clarification to ensure workshop success.
			Facilitator should ask:
			• What expectations do you have for this workshop?
			• Are there any other expectations for this workshop? Begin managing participants' expectations for the work to be completed. Document the participants' expectations on a flip chart page and post the page on the wall. These expectations will be reviewed at the close of the workshop to ensure that all expectations were met.
				• Ice breaker activity
				• Workshop agenda
				• Round robin technique to explore workshop expectations
				• Flip chart to capture workshop expectations

Figure 6-1—Business Modeling Workshop Facilitator Agenda, continued

Topic	Presenter	Allotted Time	Facilitator Agenda	Facilitation Tools and Techniques
3. Workshop ground rules	Facilitator and process team		Develop a set of team and decision-making ground rules prior to the workshop. Send the ground rules with the agenda in advance. Review the ground rules with the participants at the beginning of the workshop. **Facilitator should ask:** • Does everyone agree with the rules? • Are there any changes or additions to the rules? • Will these rules foster a collaborative and team working environment? • Are there any off-limits topics? • As a team, how should we handle any hidden agendas?	• Ground rules template • Questioning techniques • Multivote technique for approval
4. Overview of housekeeping items	Facilitator and process team		Review housekeeping items and ensure that participants understand each housekeeping item. • Facilities orientation • Breaks and lunch • Emergencies • Minimizing interruptions	

Figure 6-1—Business Modeling Workshop Facilitator Agenda, continued

Topic	Presenter	Allotted Time	Facilitator Agenda	Facilitation Tools and Techniques
5. Overview of parking boards	Facilitator and process team		Prepare parking boards in advance. Use a flip chart for each parking board and position it so that it is visible to all participants and easily accessible by the facilitator. A parking lot is a component of the parking boards. Parking boards are flip charts marked with titles that represent categories of information. They are used to capture the information during facilitated sessions in real time. A flip chart page for each type of parking board is placed on the wall to begin capturing items in the following categories: • Parking lot • Assumptions • Risks • Constraints • Issues • Action items Review the purpose of parking boards with workshop attendees. **Parking lot:** a tool to track questions that require follow-up **Issue:** a concern raised by any stakeholder that requires a decision or resolution. **Action items:** a list of follow-up actions that are assigned an owner and a timeframe for completion. **Risk:** an uncertain event or condition that, if it occurs, has a positive or negative effect on a project's objectives. **Constraint:** a restriction or limitation with which the team must comply throughout the project. **Facilitator should ask:** Are there any questions about the parking boards?	• Flip chart techniques • Parking board definitions

Figure 6-1—Business Modeling Workshop Facilitator Agenda, continued

Topic	Presenter	Allotted Time	Facilitator Agenda	Facilitation Tools and Techniques
6. Overview of process modeling guidelines	Facilitator and process team		Review the guidelines and tools for process modeling. Help participants understand the value and purpose of defining and/or improving the current business processes. Some of the benefits include: • Helps build consensus among business teams on what the process should look like • Enables teams to identify areas that need improvement • Provides a framework for organizational metrics • Helps teams identify inputs, outputs, decision points, and steps to complete a business function • Supports consistency and improves efficiencies among business teams	• Process modeling guidelines and tools
7. Review current "as is" process	Facilitator and process team		Consider the process today. Review activities that occur on a regular basis. Identify categories and subcategories of activities within the process. **Facilitator should ask:** • Is this the current process? • If not, how does this differ today? • What are the functions of this process? • Who currently supports this process? • What is the purpose of this process? • Are there any additional categories to consider? • Are there any subcategories to consider? • What are the inputs to this process? • What are the outputs of this process?	• Model of "as is" process • Flowcharting • Relationship maps • Cross-functional process maps • Sequential questioning techniques • Consensus-building techniques

Figure 6-1—Business Modeling Workshop Facilitator Agenda, continued

Topic	Presenter	Allotted Time	Facilitator Agenda	Facilitation Tools and Techniques
8. Identify the current problems and root causes	Facilitator and process team		Using the "as is" process, lead participants to identify problems within the current process. Facilitate a root cause analysis to determine the underlying causes of the identified problems. **Facilitator should ask:** • What has changed? • What needs to change? • Which function or activity is not working? • What are the apparent disconnects? • Are the steps of the process in the correct order? • Are the roles and responsibilities correctly identified and assigned? • Are the handoffs and interfaces effective? • Are the steps redundant, complex, or a cause of bottlenecks? • Are any steps unnecessary?	• SWOT technique • Cause-and-effect charting • Fishbone diagram • Breakout groups

Figure 6-1—Business Modeling Workshop Facilitator Agenda, continued

Topic	Presenter	Allotted Time	Facilitator Agenda	Facilitation Tools and Techniques
9. Define "future state" process	Facilitator and process team		Based on the identified problems and root causes, what are the opportunities to improve the process? What would the "future state" look like? **Facilitator should ask:** • What improvements would add value to the process? • What improvement would improve the quality of the work? • What changes would make the process more cost-effective? • What improvements would reduce redundancy, complexity, and bottlenecks? • What steps would improve resource allocations? • What deliverables must be developed to support the "future state" process?	• Flowcharting • Relationship maps • Cross-functional process maps • Sequential questioning techniques • Consensus-building techniques • Gap analysis technique • Decision grid • Troubleshooting work sheet

Figure 6-1—Business Modeling Workshop Facilitator Agenda, continued

Topic	Presenter	Allotted Time	Facilitator Agenda	Facilitation Tools and Techniques
10. Prioritize "future state" improvements	Facilitator and process team		List the improvements identified for the "future state" process. Review with participants. **Facilitator should ask:** • Are there any improvements to add to the list? • Is everyone in agreement with the list? • What actions are required to complete "future state" improvements? Help the participants to prioritize the list. **Facilitator should ask:** • What criteria should be considered for ranking improvements? • Are all criteria equally important or are some more important than others? Using prioritization and multivoting techniques, prioritize the improvements and assign an owner.	• Priority matrix • Multivoting techniques
11. Implementation plan	Facilitator and process team		Facilitate team to develop an implementation plan for the "future state" process. The plan should identify: • Process owner • Activities and tasks • Costs • Timeline for completion • Measures of success • Training requirements • Review and approval activities	

Figure 6-1—Business Modeling Workshop Facilitator Agenda, continued

Topic	Presenter	Allotted Time	Facilitator Agenda	Facilitation Tools and Techniques

12. Review parking boards and next steps	Facilitator		• Review the parking boards.
			• Assign a due date and owner to each action item or issue for resolution.
			• Categorize the risks and document them in the risk log.
			• Review the next steps and associated timelines. These should include:
			  • Issue resolution
			  • Action items
			  • Distribution of interview results
			• Communicate when and where the workshop results will be published for review and required follow-up.
			• Inform the interviewee of the project repository location.
			
			Facilitator should ask:
			• Are there any questions?
			• Are there any corrections to the parking board items?
			• Does the team have your commitment to complete the assigned next steps?
				• Parking board templates
				• Issues log
				• Action item log
				• Risk log
				• Constraints log
				• Parking lot
				• Project repository guidelines

Figure 6-1—Business Modeling Workshop Facilitator Agenda, continued

Topic	Presenter	Allotted Time	Facilitator Agenda	Facilitation Tools and Techniques
13. Workshop summary	Facilitator		Review the completed work. Facilitator should ask: • Are there any questions regarding the follow-up activities? • Will each assigned owner commit to the completion of the follow-up activities?	Summary techniques
14. Evaluate and close workshop	Facilitator		• Review the workshop goals and objectives. • Conduct a workshop evaluation to validate if the measures of success have been met. • Conduct a lessons learned discussion to identify ways to improve workshop performance. • Thank participants for their time and contributions.	• Workshop agenda with goals, objectives, and measures of success • Workshop evaluation form • Lessons learned template

Prototype Review Meetings

The prototype review meeting, shown in Figure 6-2, is a facilitated set of activities designed to guide key stakeholders as they review prototypes, identify prototype issues, and detail additional requirements needed to complete the product or solution.

Purpose and Benefits

+ Confirm requirements by reviewing a prototype (a mock-up of a solution or a solution component)

+ Reaches an agreement and/or consensus regarding the final solution

+ Allows a shared work product between the business and technology teams

+ Assesses the feasibility of quality requirements

+ Reduces overall project risk

+ Detects early unnecessary functionality

+ Validates the scope of work

Challenges

+ Ensuring that the right participants are present and actively participate

+ Sufficient preparation and planning time for each prototype review

+ Ensuring participation of stakeholders throughout prototype reviews

+ Effectively managing timelines for each review period

Who Should Attend

+ Project sponsor

+ Prototype team

+ Key sources for requirements, such as internal and external business users and subject matter experts

+ Project team members

Meeting Strategy

Suggestions for meeting strategy include:

+ Set expectations and establish a collaborative atmosphere.

+ Provide a thorough overview of the business need.

+ Set and accept scope boundaries.

+ Summarize and document results.

+ Plan for the next prototype review.

Roles and Responsibilities

+ **Project sponsor.** Authorizes and funds the reviews.

+ **Facilitator.** Designs, plans, and leads the review process using effective facilitation skills, tools, and techniques.

+ **Business analyst.** Often acts as the facilitator. The business analyst is a core project team member who leads stakeholder representatives to elicit, analyze, specify, validate, and manage project requirements throughout the life cycle.

- **Project team.** Contribute to the discovery of requirements and begin building relationships with key stakeholders.

- **Requirements team.** Support the discovery, analysis, and documentation of requirements. These persons work closely with business users to evolve the prototype product.

- **Business users and subject matter experts.** Contribute to the discovery of requirements needed to solve the problem.

- **Scribe.** Captures and documents the work and results of the review.

Inputs

- Documented results of previous prototype reviews

- Business case and/or project charter

- Copies of requirement hard sources for use during review activities

- Current version of requirements document

- Prototype assessment guidelines

- Prototype to be reviewed

Outputs

- Updated business requirements document

- Updated stakeholder analysis document

- Documented issues, risks, constraints, and action items

- Evolution of design and development components

- Testing results

Facilitator Agenda

A sample facilitator agenda for a prototype review meeting is shown in Figure 6-2.

Figure 6-2—Prototype Review Meeting Facilitator Agenda

General Information	
Date:	**Time:**
Subject:	**Location:**
Meeting Sponsor:	**Facilitator:**
Project Manager:	**Business Analyst:**
Project Name:	**Project ID:**
Review Objectives:	• Translate abstract theories into detailed requirements needed to complete the product design • Reach an agreement and/or consensus regarding the recommended solution • Allow a shared work product between the business and technology teams • Validate scope of work and requirements

Attendees					
Attended	**Name**	**Business Area Representing**	**Attended**	**Name**	**Business Area Representing**

Figure 6-2—Prototype Review Meeting Facilitator Agenda, continued

Topic	Presenter	Allotted Time	Facilitator Agenda	Facilitation Tools and Techniques
1. Open the prototype review session	Project sponsor or key stakeholder		Project sponsor or key stakeholder opens the review. He or she should set the tone of the review. It is important to foster an honest and positive environment to ensure a productive meeting. Open the meeting by: • Providing an overview of the business need • Reviewing goals and objectives of the proposed solution • Communicating the review's measures of success **Facilitator should ask:** • What elements of the business need require more clarification? • Are there any questions, concerns, issues, or constraints regarding the identified business need?	• Meet with project sponsor or key stakeholder in advance to review the role he or she will play during the review • Business case or project charter • Questioning techniques
2. Review ground rules	Facilitator and prototype team		• Develop a set of team and decision-making ground rules prior to the workshop. Send the ground rules with the agenda in advance. • Review the ground rules with the participants at the beginning of the review session. **Facilitator should ask:** • Does everyone agree with the rules? • Are there any changes or additions to the rules? • Will these rules foster a collaborative and team working environment? • Are there any off-limits topics? • As a team, how should we handle any hidden agendas?	• Ground rules template • Questioning techniques • Multivote technique for approval

Figure 6-2—Prototype Review Meeting Facilitator Agenda, continued

Topic	Presenter	Allotted Time	Facilitator Agenda	Facilitation Tools and Techniques

3. Introductions and expectations	Facilitator and prototype team		• Conduct an ice breaker activity to:
			  • Introduce participants to each other
			  • Begin to foster team collaboration
			• Review agenda and timeline.
			• Conduct a round robin exercise to identify participants' expectations. It is important for participants to clearly understand the purpose and work to be completed during the review. If expectations are not aligned, work toward clarification to ensure a successful review.
			Facilitator should ask:
			  • What expectations do you have for this review?
			  • Are there any other expectations for this review?
			Begin managing participants' expectations for the work to be completed. Document the participants' expectations on a flip chart page and post the page on the wall. These expectations will be revisited at the close of the review to ensure that all expectations were met.
				• Ice breaker activity
				• Review agenda
				• Round robin technique to explore expectations
				• Flip chart to capture expectations

4. Overview of housekeeping items	Facilitator and prototype team		Review housekeeping items and ensure that participants understand each housekeeping item.
			  • Facilities orientation
			  • Breaks and lunch
			  • Emergencies
			  • Minimizing interruptions	

Figure 6-2—Prototype Review Meeting Facilitator Agenda, continued

Topic	Presenter	Allotted Time	Facilitator Agenda	Facilitation Tools and Techniques
5. Overview of parking boards	Facilitator and prototype team		Prepare parking boards in advance. Use a flip chart for each parking board and position it in the room so that it is visible to all participants and easily accessed by the facilitator. A parking lot is a component of the parking boards. Parking boards are flip charts marked with titles that represent categories of information. They are used to capture the information during facilitated sessions in real time. A flip chart page for each type of parking board is placed on the wall to begin capturing items in the following categories: • Parking lot • Assumptions • Risks • Constraints • Issues • Action items Review the purpose of parking boards with workshop attendees. **Parking lot:** a tool to track questions that require follow-up. **Issue:** a concern raised by any stakeholder that requires a decision or resolution. **Action items:** a list of follow-up actions that are assigned an owner and a timeframe for completion. **Risk:** an uncertain event or condition that, if it occurs, has a positive or negative effect on a project's objectives. **Constraint:** a restriction or limitation with which the team must comply throughout the project. **Facilitator should ask:** • Are there any questions about the parking boards?	• Flip chart techniques • Parking board definitions • Questioning techniques

Figure 6-2—Prototype Review Meeting Facilitator Agenda, continued

Topic	Presenter	Allotted Time	Facilitator Agenda	Facilitation Tools and Techniques
6. Overview of prototype process	Facilitator and prototype team		Ensure that participants understand the value of the prototype process. Discuss such benefits as: • Helps build consensus among business teams on what the product should look like • Formulates abstract concepts into more concrete ideas • Ensures a collaboration of all affected teams • Improves resource, time, and cost impacts by ensuring that users focus on the right requirements • Provides a more targeted solution Review the prototype process and current status. Help participants understand the: • Purpose of the review • Overview of prototype approach (throw-away or evolutionary) • Roles and responsibilities during the review • Overview of the current prototype status • Guidelines for prototype review Review business and technical environmental constraints. **Facilitator should ask:** • What are the benefits of a prototype approach? • What value will this review bring to the final solution? • Does everyone commit to the process?	• Prototype overview • Prototype status report • Prototype process, guidelines, and tools • Questioning techniques

Figure 6-2—Prototype Review Meeting Facilitator Agenda, continued

Topic	Presenter	Allotted Time	Facilitator Agenda	Facilitation Tools and Techniques
7. Demonstrate or simulate the prototype for review	Facilitator and prototype team		Conduct a demonstration or simulation of each prototype component to review. Ensure that you view the components of the prototype in sequence. The facilitator should begin recording and identifying: • Issues and recommendations • Risks and constraints • Affected areas of the business requirements document, models, use cases, and business rules	• Prototype review checklists • Prototype review worksheet template • Parking board templates • Discussion techniques • Questioning techniques
8. Assess prototype by scope/requirement category	Facilitator		Assess each scope/requirements category independently. **Facilitator should ask:** • What works well? • What needs improvement? • How should we improve? • What is the impact of the improvement? • Who is affected by the improvement? Document findings, results, and parking boards.	• Current requirements Document • Prototype assessment Guidelines • List of scope categories • Parking boards
9. Summarize prototype review	Facilitator		Provide summary of findings. **Facilitator should ask:** • Is there anything else to add? • Are there any changes or revisions to the documented results? Review next steps and associated timelines. Communicate when and where the results will be published.	• Post completed work on the wall for discussion • Repository guidelines • Communication plan

Figure 6-2—Prototype Review Meeting Facilitator Agenda, continued

Topic	Presenter	Allotted Time	Facilitator Agenda	Facilitation Tools and Techniques

10. Review parking boards and next steps	Facilitator		• Review the parking boards.
			• Assign a due date and owner to each action item or issue for resolution.
			• Review next steps and associated timelines. These should include:
			  • Issues resolution
			  • Action items
			  • Distribution of review results
			• Communicate when and where the review results will be published.
			• Inform the interviewee of the project repository location.
			Facilitator should ask:
			  • Are there any questions?
			  • Are there any corrections to the parking board items?
			  • Does the team have your commitment to complete the assigned next steps?
				• Parking board templates
				• Issues log
				• Action item log
				• Risk log
				• Constraints log
				• Parking lot
				• Project repository guidelines

11. Evaluate and close prototype review	Facilitator and prototype team		• Review the goals and objectives. • Conduct an evaluation to validate whether the measures of success for the prototype session have been met. • Conduct a lessons learned discussion to identify ways to improve future reviews. • Thank participants for their time and contributions.	• Agenda with goals, objectives and measures of success • Evaluation form or technique • Lessons learned template

Risk Management Workshops

A risk management workshop is a facilitated set of activities designed to guide stakeholders as they work toward the identification and assessment of project risks. The purpose is to monitor and control risk events throughout the project life cycle. As Requirements begin to mature, it is wise for the project manager and business analyst to conduct a risk management workshop focusing on requirement risks and risks to the business.

Purpose and Benefits

+ Collaboratively work as a team to identify and assess possible project risks

+ Learn the risk management process and supporting tools and techniques

+ Build stakeholder awareness of potential risks and risk response strategies

+ Foster a proactive approach to risk management

Challenges

+ Ensuring that the right participants are present and actively participate

+ Securing sufficient preparation and planning time for the workshop

+ Enlisting a skilled facilitator using appropriate facilitation tools and techniques

+ Selling the benefits of proactive risk management to project stakeholders

Who Should Attend?

- Project team

- Key project stakeholders

- Project sponsor

- Business users and subject matter experts

Meeting Strategy

- Hands-on workshop to complete risk management activities

- Break-out sessions in small teams

- Completion of a risk register for high-priority risks

Roles and Responsibilities

- **Project sponsor.** Authorizes and funds the workshop.

- **Facilitator.** Designs, plans, and leads the workshop process using effective facilitation skills, tools, and techniques.

- **Project team.** Contribute to the identification and assessment of potential project risks.

- **Business users and subject matter experts.** Contribute to the discovery of risks in each area of expertise.

- **Scribe.** Captures and documents the work and results of the workshop.

- **Project Manager.** Leads and/or facilitates the risk management workshop.

Inputs

+ Risk management process, tools, and techniques

+ Risk management plan

+ Workshop ground rules for team participation, decision-making, and brainstorming

+ Sources for risk identification

Outputs

+ Completed risk breakdown structure with identified risk sources and categories

+ Updated risk register with assigned owner, priority, and risk statement

+ Risk worksheet for each identified risk

Facilitator Agenda

A sample facilitator agenda for a risk management workshop is shown in Figure 6-3.

Figure 6-3—Risk Management Workshop Facilitator Agenda

General Information

Date:	Time:
Subject:	Location:
Meeting Sponsor:	Facilitator:
Project Manager:	Business Analyst:
Project Name:	Project ID:
Review Objectives:	• Collaboratively work as a team to identify and assess possible requirements and/or business risks • Learn the risk management process and supporting tools and techniques • Build stakeholder awareness of potential risks • Foster a proactive approach to risk management

Attendees

Attended	Name	Business Area Representing	Attended	Name	Business Area Representing

Figure 6-3—Risk Management Workshop Facilitator Agenda, continued

Topic	Presenter	Allotted Time	Facilitator Agenda	Facilitation Tools and Techniques
1. Open risk workshop	Project sponsor or key stakeholder		Project sponsor or key stakeholder opens the workshop. He or she should set the tone of the workshop. It is key to foster an honest and positive environment to ensure a productive meeting. Open the meeting by: • Providing an overview of the business need • Reviewing workshop goals and objectives • Communicating workshop measures of success **Facilitator should ask:** • What elements of the business need require more clarification? • Are there any questions, concerns, issues, or constraints with the identified business need?	• Meet with project sponsor or key stakeholder in advance to review the role he or she will play during the workshop • Business case or project charter • Questioning techniques

Figure 6-3—Risk Management Workshop Facilitator Agenda, continued

Topic	Presenter	Allotted Time	Facilitator Agenda	Facilitation Tools and Techniques

2. Workshop overview, introductions, and expectations	Facilitator		• Conduct an ice breaker activity to:
			  • Introduce participants to each other.
			  • Begin to foster team collaboration.
			• Review workshop agenda and timeline.
			• Review interview roles and responsibilities.
			• Conduct a round robin exercise to identify participants' expectations. It is key for participants to clearly understand the purpose and work to be completed during the workshop. If expectations are not aligned, work toward clarification to ensure workshop success.
			Facilitator should ask:
			• What expectations do you have for this workshop?
			• Are there any other expectations for this workshop?
			Begin managing participants' expectations for the work to be completed. Document the participants' expectations on a flip chart page and post the page on the wall. These expectations will be reviewed at the close of the workshop to ensure that all expectations were met.
				• Ice breaker activity
				• Workshop agenda
				• Round robin technique to explore workshop expectations
				• Flip chart to capture workshop expectations

Figure 6-3—Risk Management Workshop Facilitator Agenda, continued

Topic	Presenter	Allotted Time	Facilitator Agenda	Facilitation Tools and Techniques
3. Workshop ground rules	Facilitator		Develop a set of team and decision-making ground rules prior to the workshop. Send the ground rules with the agenda in advance. Review the ground rules with participants at the beginning of the workshop. **Facilitator should ask:** • Does everyone agree with the rules? • Are there any changes or additions to the rules? • Will these rules foster a collaborative and team working environment? • Are there any off-limits topics? • As a team, how should we handle any hidden agendas?	• Ground rules template • Questioning techniques • Multivote technique for approval
4. Overview of housekeeping items	Facilitator		Review housekeeping items and ensure that participants understand each housekeeping item. • Facilities orientation • Breaks and lunch • Emergencies • Minimizing interruptions	

Figure 6-3—Risk Management Workshop Facilitator Agenda, continued

Topic	Presenter	Allotted Time	Facilitator Agenda	Facilitation Tools and Techniques
5. Review risk management plan	Facilitator		Provide overview of the risk management plan, including an overview of the: • Risk management process • Deliverables • Tools • Risk management team • Monitoring and control activities • Maintenance and storage of risk documents **Facilitator should ask:** • What are the benefits of a risk management plan? • What value will this plan bring to the project? • Are there any suggestions for changes or improvement of the plan? • Does everyone commit to the risk management plan?	• Risk management process document • Questioning techniques • Consensus-building techniques

Figure 6-3—Risk Management Workshop Facilitator Agenda, continued

Topic	Presenter	Allotted Time	Facilitator Agenda	Facilitation Tools and Techniques
6. Overview of parking boards	Facilitator		Prepare parking boards in advance. Use a flip chart for each parking board and position it in the room so that it is visible to all participants and easily accessible by the facilitator. A parking lot is a component of the parking boards. Parking boards are flip charts marked with titles that represent categories of information. They are used to capture the information during facilitated sessions in real time. A flip chart page for each type of parking board is placed on the wall to begin capturing items in the following categories: • Parking lot • Assumptions • Risks • Constraints • Issues • Action items Review the purpose of parking boards with workshop attendees. **Parking lot:** a tool to track questions that require follow-up. **Issue:** a concern raised by any stakeholder that requires a decision or resolution. **Action items:** a list of follow-up actions that are assigned an owner and a timeframe for completion. **Risk:** an uncertain event or condition that, if it occurs, has a positive or negative effect on a project's objectives. **Constraint:** a restriction or limitation with which the team must comply throughout the project. **Facilitator should ask:** • Are there any questions about the parking boards?	• Flip chart techniques • Parking board definitions

Figure 6-3—Risk Management Workshop Facilitator Agenda, continued

Topic	Presenter	Allotted Time	Facilitator Agenda	Facilitation Tools and Techniques
7. Risk breakdown structure (RBS)	Facilitator		A risk breakdown structure (RBS) is a source-oriented grouping of project risk events that organizes and defines the sources of risks to the project. Prior to the workshop, work with individuals and small teams to develop a straw man RBS that identifies sources of risks and is organized into categories and subcategories. Prepare the hard sources that will be used to identify categories of risk and send them in advance. Examples: • Project work breakdown structure (Project WBS) • Project documents (past and present) • Process documents • System documents • Training documents Review the straw man RBS with workshop participants. **Facilitator should ask:** • Are there any additional categories of risks to add to the RBS? • Are the risks categorized into logical and manageable groupings? • Can each grouping be assigned a risk event owner?	• Example of a risk breakdown structure (RBS) • Straw man of an RBS • Hard sources for risk identification • Project risk checklist • Questioning techniques • Brainstorming techniques • Breakout groups

Figure 6-3—Risk Management Workshop Facilitator Agenda, continued

Topic	Presenter	Allotted Time	Facilitator Agenda	Facilitation Tools and Techniques
8. Workshop summary			Reconvene the focus groups to review the completed work. Discuss the follow-up risk management activities for each assigned risk event. • The risk owner of each risk event, supported by key stakeholders and/or subject matter experts, should decide how to respond to the risk. • The risk owner will work with teams to develop mitigation and/or contingency plans. • The risk owner and supporting team will identify triggers for each risk event. • Obtain a timeline commitment from each risk owner to complete and publish the follow-up activities. **Facilitator should ask:** • Are there any questions regarding the follow-up activities? • Will each risk owner commit to the completion of the follow-up activities?	• Summary techniques • Risk response planning guidelines
9. Review next steps	Facilitator		• Review next steps and associated timelines. • Communicate when the risk log and risk worksheets with risk responses and plans will be completed and published for team review.	• Repository guidelines • Communication plan

Figure 6-3—Risk Management Workshop Facilitator Agenda, continued

Topic	Presenter	Allotted Time	Facilitator Agenda	Facilitation Tools and Techniques

10. Review parking boards and next steps	Facilitator		• Review the parking boards.
			• Assign and timeline each action item or issue for resolution.
			• Categorize the risks and document them in the risk log.
			• Review next steps and associated timelines. This should include:
			  • Issues resolution
			  • Action items
			  • Distribution of interview results
			• Communicate when and where the workshop results will be published for review and required follow-up.
			• Inform the interviewee of the project repository location.
			Facilitator should ask:
			  • Are there any questions?
			  • Are there any corrections to the parking board items?
			  • Does the team have your commitment to complete the assigned next steps?
				• Parking board templates
				• Issues log
				• Action item log
				• Risk log
				• Constraints log
				• Parking lot
				• Project repository guidelines

11. Evaluate and close workshop	Facilitator		• Review the workshop goals and objectives. • Conduct a workshop evaluation to validate whether the measures of success have been met. • Conduct a lessons learned discussion to identify ways to improve workshop performance. • Thank participants for their time and contributions.	• Workshop agenda with goals, objectives, and measures of success • Workshop evaluation form • Lessons learned template

Chapter 7

Requirements Specification Review Meetings

In This Chapter:

- Challenges

- Types of Meetings

- Requirements Specification Review Meeting

The specification of what is to be accomplished supplements the scoping and analysis models. During the process of specifying what is needed, the business analyst continues to work collaboratively with the customers and end-users of the new solution and with key members of the solution development team. One or more text deliverables might result from this step. Typically the specification documents are the user requirements document and the software requirements specification document. Other requirements specifications include the requirements document, business requirements document, use case document, concept of operations (ConOps), requirements definition, requirements statement, system definition, functional specification, supplemental specification, and technical specification. Minimally, a business requirements document is created.

In addition to drafting the business requirements documentation, requirements specification involves progressively elaborating, refining, and organizing the requirements into a structured set of requirement artifacts. As requirements are documented during this activity, they are continually validated by both the business and technical teams.

Requirement specifications are elaborated from and linked to the structured models, providing a repository of requirements with a complete attribute set. Please refer to *Getting it Right: Business Requirements Analysis Tools and Techniques* for a complete discussion of requirement specification activities.

The value of the business requirements documentation is that it (1) provides text detail for information not represented in the scoping and analysis models, (2) drives consensus among various stakeholder groups on what the new system must do, (3) serves as a vehicle to obtain agreement on the part of the business and technical teams that the business need is understood, and (4) serves as a bridge between business and system requirements.[1] Attributes allow the requirements team to associate information with individual or related groups of requirements and often facilitate the requirements analysis process by filtering and sorting.

Challenges

The challenges to requirements specifications meetings include:

+ Identifying the appropriate participants

+ Determining the list of attributes to be used

Types of Meetings

The meeting discussed in detail in this chapter is the requirements specification review meeting.

Requirements Specification Review Meeting

The requirements specification review meeting, shown in Figure 7-1, is a facilitated set of activities designed to guide stakeholders through the review of the requirements specification document(s).

Purpose and Benefits

+ Ensures that the business view is transformed correctly into the technical view

+ Makes certain the requirements are transformed into precise and clear text statements

+ Detects quality issues in the document before the requirements are transitioned to the design team

Challenges

+ Securing effective and skilled facilitation

+ Securing sufficient time for advance preparation and planning

+ Securing the right stakeholders to participate

+ Determining when the business requirements are stable enough for the review

+ Managing the various perspectives that might produce different review results

Who Should Attend?

- Project team

- Key project stakeholders

- Project sponsor

- Business users

- Subject matter experts

- Vendors (as appropriate)

Meeting Strategy

- The requirements specification review takes place when the requirements team has completed and documented a thorough set of requirements specifications that cover all aspects of the solution.

- The requirements specification document is sent out in advance for review and preparation for the meeting.

- The requirements specification document inspection checklist is provided to guide the participants and improve the quality of the review.

- Ongoing reviews are conducted until the final requirements specification document is approved, baselined, and transitioned to the design team.

Roles and Responsibilities

+ **Project sponsor.** Authorizes and funds the review.

+ **Facilitator.** Designs, plans, and leads the review process using structured facilitation tools and techniques.

+ **Requirements team.** Works to develop and prepare the requirements specification for review.

+ **Business analyst.** Ensures that the business view is transformed effectively into the technical view, participates in the review, updates the business requirements document and the requirements traceability matrix, and acts as a liaison between the technical team and the business customer.

+ **Business users and subject matter experts.** Review the document and provide recommendations or approval of the document.

+ **Scribe.** Captures and documents the results of the review and the parking boards.

Inputs

+ A fully drafted requirements specification document

+ A completed requirements traceability matrix

+ Review guidelines and checklist

+ Requirement analysis models, diagrams, and tables

+ Stakeholder list

+ Review training and tools

+ Business rules, regulations, and standards

+ Hard and soft sources used for requirements elicitation

Outputs

+ An approved requirements specification document

+ Updated business analysis models, diagrams, and tables

+ Updated stakeholder list

Facilitator Agenda

A sample facilitator agenda for a requirements specification review meeting is shown in Figure 7-1.

Figure 7-1—Requirements Specification Review Meeting Facilitator Agenda

General Information	
Date:	**Time:**
Subject:	**Location:**
Meeting Sponsor:	**Facilitator:**
Project Manager:	**Business Analyst:**
Project Name:	**Project ID:**
Review Objectives:	• Confirm that the business view is transformed correctly into the technical view • Inspect the user and system requirements to verify that they are transformed into precise and clear text statements • Detect quality issues in the document before the requirements are transitioned to the design team

Attendees					
Attended	**Name**	**Business Area Representing**	**Attended**	**Name**	**Business Area Representing**

Figure 7-1—Requirements Specification Review Meeting Facilitator Agenda, continued

Topic	Presenter	Allotted Time	Facilitator Agenda	Facilitation Tools and Techniques
1. Open the meeting	Project sponsor or key stakeholder		Project sponsor or important stakeholder will open the review. He or she should set the tone of the review. It is important to foster an honest and positive environment to ensure a productive meeting. Open the meeting by: • Providing an overview of the business need • Reviewing goals and objectives of the proposed solution • Communicating the review's measures of success **Facilitator should ask:** • What elements of the business need require more clarification? • Are there any questions, concerns, issues, or constraints regarding the identified business need?	• Meet with project sponsor or key stakeholder in advance to review the role he or she will play during the review • Business case or project charter • Questioning techniques
2. Review ground rules	Facilitator and review team		Develop a set of team and decision-making ground rules prior to review session. Send the ground rules with the agenda in advance. Review the ground rules with participants at the beginning of the review session. **Facilitator should ask:** • Does everyone agree with the rules? • Are there any changes or additions to the rules? • Will these rules foster a collaborative and team working environment? • Are there any off-limits topics? • As a team, how should we handle any hidden agendas?	• Ground rules template • Questioning techniques • Multivote technique for approval

Note: Actual agenda items will depend on the sections contained in the requirements specification document under review.

Figure 7-1—Requirements Specification Review Meeting Facilitator Agenda, continued

Topic	Presenter	Allotted Time	Facilitator Agenda	Facilitation Tools and Techniques

3. Introductions and expectations	Facilitator and review team		• Conduct an ice breaker activity to:
			  • Introduce participants to each other
			  • Begin to foster team collaboration
			• Review agenda and timeline
			• Conduct a round robin exercise to identify participants' expectations. It is important for participants to clearly understand the purpose and work to be completed during the review. If expectations are not aligned, work toward clarification to ensure a successful review.
			Facilitator should ask:
			  • What expectations do you have for this review?
			  • Are there any other expectations for this review?
			Begin managing participants' expectations for the work to be completed. Document the participants' expectations on a flip chart page and post the page on the wall. These expectations will be revisited at the close of the review to ensure that all expectations were met.
				• Ice breaker activity
				• Review agenda
				• Round robin technique to explore participants' expectations
				• Flip chart to capture expectations

4. Overview of housekeeping items	Facilitator and review team		Review housekeeping items and ensure that participants understand each housekeeping item.
			  • Facilities orientation
			  • Breaks and lunch
			  • Emergencies
			  • Minimizing interruptions	

Figure 7-1—Requirements Specification Review Meeting Facilitator Agenda, continued

Topic	Presenter	Allotted Time	Facilitator Agenda	Facilitation Tools and Techniques
5. Overview of parking boards	Facilitator and review team		Prepare parking boards in advance. Use a flip chart for each parking board and position it in the room so that it is visible to all participants and easily accessed by the facilitator. A parking lot is a component of the parking boards. Parking boards are flip charts marked with titles that represent categories of information. They are used to capture the information during facilitated sessions in real time. A flip chart page for each type of parking board is placed on the wall to begin capturing items in the following categories: • Parking lot • Assumptions • Risks • Constraints • Issues • Action items Review the purpose of parking boards with workshop attendees. **Parking lot:** a tool to track questions that require follow-up. **Issue:** a concern raised by any stakeholder that requires a decision or resolution. **Action items:** a list of follow-up actions that are assigned an owner and a timeframe for completion. **Risk:** an uncertain event or condition that, if it occurs, has a positive or negative effect on a project's objectives. **Constraint:** a restriction or limitation with which the team must comply throughout the project. **Facilitator should ask:** • Are there any questions about the parking boards?	• Flip chart techniques • Parking board definitions • Questioning techniques

Figure 7-1—Requirements Specification Review Meeting Facilitator Agenda, continued

Topic	Presenter	Allotted Time	Facilitator Agenda	Facilitation Tools and Techniques
6. Overview of requirements specification document(s)	Facilitator and review team		Review the following areas of the document for completeness, accuracy, and clarity. Identify defects and recommendations for improvement. • Product overview • Impacted stakeholders and users • Product features • Product documentation • Product risks, constraints, and assumptions • Business and technical dependencies **Facilitator should ask:** • Are there any corrections or recommendations?	• Review process overview • Draft requirements specification document • Checklist and supporting tools • Questioning techniques

Figure 7-1—Requirements Specification Review Meeting Facilitator Agenda, continued

Topic	Presenter	Allotted Time	Facilitator Agenda	Facilitation Tools and Techniques

7. Functional requirements	Facilitator and review team		• Review each category of functional requirement and discuss recommendations for improvement or detected errors. Use the questions in the inspection checklist to review each requirement for:
			  • Accuracy
			  • Clarity
			  • Ambiguity
			  • Consistency
			  • Dependencies
			  • Feasibility
			  • Testability
			• Document findings, results, and parking boards.
			• Trace each requirement and document it on the requirements traceability matrix (RTM).
			Facilitator should ask:
			  • Have any defects been identified?
			  • What improvements are needed?
			  • Who will make the improvement?
			  • Have all the quality attributes been identified?
			  • Is the requirement properly numbered and labeled?
			  • Is each requirement allocated to the correct resource?
			  • Have any constraints been identified?
			  • What assumptions are being made?
			  • Have any risks been identified?
			  • Have any business rules been identified?
				• Approved requirements document
				• Quality attribute table
				• Inspection checklist

Figure 7-1—Requirements Specification Review Meeting Facilitator Agenda, continued

Topic	Presenter	Allotted Time	Facilitator Agenda	Facilitation Tools and Techniques
8. External interface require-ments	Facilitator and review team		• Review each category of functional requirement and discuss recommendations for improvement or detected errors. Use the questions in the inspection checklist to review each requirement for: • Accuracy • Clarity • Ambiguity • Consistency • Dependencies • Feasibility • Testability • Document findings, results, and parking boards. • Trace and document each requirement to the RTM. **Facilitator should ask:** • Have any defects been identified? • What improvements are needed? • Who will make the improvements? • Have all the quality attributes been identified? • Is each requirement properly numbered and labeled? • Is each requirement allocated to the correct resource? • Have any constraints been identified? • What assumptions are being made? • Have any risks been identified? • Have any business rules been identified?	• Approved requirements document • Quality attribute table • Inspection checklist

Figure 7-1—Requirements Specification Review Meeting Facilitator Agenda, continued

Topic	Presenter	Allotted Time	Facilitator Agenda	Facilitation Tools and Techniques

9. User interface require-ments	Facilitator and review team		• Review each category of functional requirement and discuss recommendations for improvement or detected errors. Use the questions in the inspection checklist to review each requirement for:
			  • Accuracy
			  • Clarity
			  • Ambiguity
			  • Consistency
			  • Dependencies
			  • Feasibility
			  • Testability
			• Document findings, results, and parking boards.
			• Trace each requirement and document it on the RTM.
			Facilitator should ask:
			• Have any defects been identified?
			• What improvements are needed?
			• Who will make the improvements?
			• Have all the quality attributes been identified?
			• Is each requirement properly numbered and labeled?
			• Is each requirement allocated to the correct resource?
			• Have any constraints been identified?
			• What assumptions are being made?
			• Have any risks been identified?
			• Have any business rules been identified?
				• Approved requirements document
				• Quality attribute table
				• Inspection checklist

Figure 7-1—Requirements Specification Review Meeting Facilitator Agenda, continued

Topic	Presenter	Allotted Time	Facilitator Agenda	Facilitation Tools and Techniques

			• Review each category of functional requirement and discuss recommendations for improvement or detected errors. Use the questions in the inspection checklist to review each requirement for:
			  • Accuracy
			  • Clarity
			  • Ambiguity
			  • Consistency
			  • Dependencies
			  • Feasibility
			  • Testability	

10. Hardware requirements	Facilitator and review team		• Document findings, results, and parking boards. • Trace each requirement and document it on the RTM. **Facilitator should ask:** • Have any defects been identified? • What improvements are needed? • Who will make the improvements? • Have all the quality attributes been identified? • Is each requirement properly numbered and labeled? • Is each requirement allocated to the correct resource? • Have any constraints been identified? • What assumptions are being made? • Have any risks been identified? • Have any business rules been identified?	• Approved requirements document • Quality attribute table • Inspection checklist

Figure 7-1—Requirements Specification Review Meeting Facilitator Agenda, continued

Topic	Presenter	Allotted Time	Facilitator Agenda	Facilitation Tools and Techniques

11. Software requirements	Facilitator and review team		• Review each category of functional requirement and discuss recommendations for improvement or detected errors. Use the questions in the inspection checklist to review each requirement for:
			  • Accuracy
			  • Clarity
			  • Ambiguity
			  • Consistency
			  • Dependencies
			  • Feasibility
			  • Testability
			• Document findings, results, and parking lots.
			• Trace each requirement and document it on the RTM.
			Facilitator should ask:
			• Have any defects been identified?
			• What improvements are needed?
			• Who will make the improvements?
			• Have all the quality attributes been identified?
			• Is each requirement properly numbered and labeled?
			• Is each requirement allocated to the correct resource?
			• Have any constraints been identified?
			• What assumptions are being made?
			• Have any risks been identified?
			• Have any business rules been identified?
				• Approved requirements document
				• Quality attribute table
				• Inspection checklist

Figure 7-1—Requirements Specification Review Meeting Facilitator Agenda, continued

Topic	Presenter	Allotted Time	Facilitator Agenda	Facilitation Tools and Techniques

12. Review parking boards and next steps	Facilitator		• Review the parking boards.
			• Assign a due date and owner to each action item or issue for resolution.
			• Review next steps and associated timelines. This should include:
			  • Issues resolution
			  • Action items
			  • Distribution of review results
			• Communicate when and where the review results will be published.
			• Inform the interviewee of the project repository location.
			Facilitator should ask:
			• Are there any questions?
			• Are there any corrections to the parking board items?
			• Does the team have your commitment to complete the assigned next steps?
				• Parking board templates
				• Issues log
				• Action item log
				• Risk log
				• Constraints log
				• Parking lot
				• Project repository guidelines

13. Summarize review	Facilitator		• Provide summary of findings. • Review next steps and associated timelines. • Communicate when and where the results will be published. **Facilitator should ask:** • Is there anything else to add? • Are there any changes or revisions to the documented results? • Do we have the commitment from participants to complete the follow-up actions?	• Post completed work on the wall for discussion • Repository guidelines • Communication plan

Figure 7-1—Requirements Specification Review Meeting Facilitator Agenda, continued

Topic	Presenter	Allotted Time	Facilitator Agenda	Facilitation Tools and Techniques
14. Evaluate and close review	Facilitator and review team		• Review the goals and objectives. • Conduct an evaluation to validate whether the measures of success for the prototype session have been met. • Conduct a lessons learned discussion to identify ways to improve future reviews. • Thank participants for their time and contributions.	• Agenda with goals, objectives, and measures of success • Evaluation form or technique • Lessons learned template

Endnote

1. Ellen Gottesdiener. *The Software Requirements Memory Jogger*, 2006. Salem, NH: GOAL/QPC.

Chapter 8

Deliverable Verification and Validation Meetings

In This Chapter:

- Challenges

- Types of Meetings

- Deliverable Inspection Meeting

Verification and validation are the processes of evaluating work products to determine whether they satisfy the business needs and are built according to specifications.

A major control gate review for projects occurs upon exiting the requirements phase and transitioning to the design phase. All requirement artifacts are presented to management for review and approval at a formal control gate review session. At this point, the project schedule, cost, and scope estimates are updated, and the business case is revisited, to provide the salient information needed to determine whether continued investment in the project is warranted. Upon securing approval to proceed, the business analyst baselines the requirements, implements a formal requirements change control process, and transitions into requirements management activities in support of solution design efforts. At the conclusion of the requirements phase, a make or buy decision is made whether to outsource the solution design and development or do the work in-house. If the work is to be outsourced, a Request for Quote (RFQ) is developed and issued. As the project moves into the design, construction, and test phases, verification and validation sessions are conducted throughout the business solution life cycle (BSLC).

Verification and validation meetings ensure that work products are complete and ready to move into the next phase of the BSLC.

Challenges

The business analyst's challenge when validating work products is to present the appropriate level of detail for review and approval.

- Requirements validation meetings are generally held from the bottom up:

  - First, conduct validation reviews of detailed requirements with users and developers.

  - Then, conduct validation reviews of project scope and high-level requirements with key business and technical managers.

  - Finally, conduct the formal phase exit control gate review with the project sponsor and other business and technical executives.

- Design, construction, and test verification meetings are conducted throughout the life cycle and are usually facilitated by the technical lead.

- The business analyst plans and facilitates the user acceptance test, the final validation that the solution satisfies the business requirements.

Types of Meetings

A typical deliverable inspection meeting is discussed in detail in this chapter.

Deliverable Inspection Meeting

A deliverable inspection meeting, shown in Figure 8-1, is a facilitated set of activities that are designed to guide stakeholders through a process to inspect a work product or project deliverable(s). The inspection looks for errors, ambiguities, and inconsistencies and attempts to improve the quality of the product and the performance of the solution.

Purpose and Benefits

+ Improves quality and understanding of the deliverable

+ Identifies and manages stakeholders' expectations

+ Validates that the deliverable will support the final solution

+ Identifies areas of high risk

+ Educates the project team and key stakeholders

+ Detects quality issues early in the development of the deliverable

Challenges

+ Securing effective and skilled facilitation

+ Securing sufficient time for advance preparation and planning

+ Ensuring that the right stakeholders participate

+ Managing the various perspectives, which can produce different review results

Who Should Attend?

+ Project team

+ Key project stakeholders

+ Project sponsor

+ Business users

+ Subject matter experts

+ Vendors (as appropriate)

Meeting Strategy

+ Identify the deliverable(s) to review.

+ Develop the participant list for the review.

+ Conduct the review through facilitated discussions using review checklists to prompt recommendations and detection of errors.

+ Revise the deliverable or work product on the basis of the recommendations of the review participants.

+ Conduct subsequent reviews if required.

Roles and Responsibilities

+ **Project sponsor.** Authorizes and funds the review.

+ **Facilitator.** Designs, plans, and leads the review process using structured facilitation tools and techniques.

+ **Technical team.** Supports the review process.

+ **Business analyst.** Participates in the review, updates business documents, and acts as a liaison between the technical team and the business customer.

+ **Business users and subject matter experts.** Participate in the review, provide recommendations, and approve the document.

+ **Scribe.** Captures and documents the results of the review and the parking boards.

Inputs

+ An approved business requirements document

+ Requirement analysis models, diagrams, and tables

+ Updated requirements traceability matrix (RTM)

+ Review guidelines and checklist

+ Stakeholder list

+ Business rules, regulations, and standards

+ Project and product documentation

+ Deliverables or work products to be reviewed

Outputs

+ Review results and areas of improvement

+ Completed deliverables

+ Updated documents, models, tables, and matrices

+ Updated stakeholder list

Facilitator Agenda

A sample facilitator agenda for a deliverable inspection meeting is shown in Figure 8-1.

Figure 8-1—Deliverable Inspection Meeting Facilitator Agenda

General Information			
Date:		Time:	
Subject:		Location:	
Meeting Sponsor:		Facilitator:	
Project Manager:		Business Analyst:	
Project Name:		Project ID:	
Review Objectives:	To conduct a quality review of a work product to detect and correct errors early in the project		

Attendees			
Attended	Name	Business Area Representing	
Attended	Name	Business Area Representing	

Figure 8-1—Deliverable Inspection Meeting Facilitator Agenda, continued

Topic	Presenter	Allotted Time	Facilitator Agenda	Facilitation Tools and Techniques
1. Open inspection session	Project sponsor or key stakeholder		Project sponsor or important stakeholder will open the review. He or she should set the tone of the review. It is important to foster an honest and positive environment to ensure a productive meeting. Open the meeting by: • Providing an overview of the business need • Reviewing goals and objectives of the proposed solution • Communicating the inspection's measures of success **Facilitator should ask:** • What elements of the business need require more clarification? • Are there any questions, concerns, issues, or constraints regarding the identified business need?	• Meet with project sponsor or key stakeholder in advance to review the role he or she will play during the review • Business case or project charter • Questioning techniques
2. Review ground rules	Facilitator and review team		Develop a set of team and decision-making ground rules prior to review session. Send the ground rules with the agenda in advance. Review the ground rules with participants at the beginning of the review session. **Facilitator should ask:** • Does everyone agree with the rules? • Are there any changes or additions to the rules? • Will these rules foster a collaborative and team working environment? • Are there any off-limits topics? • As a team, how should we handle any hidden agendas?	• Ground rules template • Questioning techniques • Multivote technique for approval

Figure 8-1—Deliverable Inspection Meeting Facilitator Agenda, continued

Topic	Presenter	Allotted Time	Facilitator Agenda	Facilitation Tools and Techniques

3. Introductions and expectations	Facilitator and review team		• Conduct an ice breaker activity to:
			  • Introduce participants to each other
			  • Begin to foster team collaboration
			• Review agenda and timeline.
			• Conduct a round robin exercise to identify participants' expectations. It is important for participants to clearly understand the purpose and work to be completed during the review. If expectations are not aligned, work toward clarification to ensure a successful review.
			Facilitator should ask:
			• What expectations do you have for this review?
			• Are there any other expectations for this review?
			Begin managing participants' expectations for the work to be completed. Document the participants' expectations on a flip chart page and post the page on the wall. These expectations will be revisited at the close of the review to ensure that all expectations were met.
				• Ice breaker activity
				• Review agenda
				• Round robin technique to explore participants' expectations
				• Flip chart to capture expectations

4. Overview of housekeeping items	Facilitator and review team		Review housekeeping items and ensure that participants understand each housekeeping item. • Facilities orientation • Breaks and lunch • Emergencies • Minimizing interruptions	

Figure 8-1—Deliverable Inspection Meeting Facilitator Agenda, continued

Topic	Presenter	Allotted Time	Facilitator Agenda	Facilitation Tools and Techniques
5. Overview of parking boards	Facilitator and review team		Prepare parking boards in advance. Use a flip chart for each parking board and position it in the room so that it is visible to all participants and easily accessed by the facilitator. A parking lot is a component of the parking boards. Parking boards are flip charts marked with titles that represent categories of information. They are used to capture the information during facilitated sessions in real time. A flip chart page for each type of parking board is placed on the wall to begin capturing items in the following categories: • Parking lot • Assumptions • Risks • Constraints • Issues • Action items Review the purpose of parking board s with workshop attendees. **Parking lot:** a tool to track questions that require follow-up. **Issue:** a concern raised by any stakeholder that requires a decision or resolution. **Action items:** a list of follow-up actions that are assigned an owner and a timeframe for completion. **Risk:** an uncertain event or condition that, if it occurs, has a positive or negative effect on a project's objectives. **Constraint:** a restriction or limitation with which the team must comply throughout the project. **Facilitator should ask:** • Are there any questions about the parking boards?	• Flip chart techniques • Parking board definitions • Questioning techniques

Figure 8-1—Deliverable Inspection Meeting Facilitator Agenda, continued

Topic	Presenter	Allotted Time	Facilitator Agenda	Facilitation Tools and Techniques
6. Overview of inspection	Facilitator and review team		Provide an overview of the following areas of the work product or deliverable to be inspected: • Overview of business need • Purpose of deliverable or work product • Background information • Current situation • Proposed solution • Impacted business areas • Impacted stakeholders • Impacted policies and business rules • Impacted systems, software, and hardware • Identified risks, constraints, and assumptions • Business and technical dependencies **Facilitator should ask:** • Are there any corrections or recommendations? • How should the work product/deliverable be improved?	• Inspection process • Inspection roles and responsibilities • Product to inspect • Inspection checklist and supporting tools • Questioning techniques • Discussion techniques

Figure 8-1—Deliverable Inspection Meeting Facilitator Agenda, continued

Topic	Presenter	Allotted Time	Facilitator Agenda	Facilitation Tools and Techniques
7. Conduct inspection	Facilitator and review team		• Inspect each component of the work product or deliverable and discuss recommendations for improvement or detected errors • Use the inspection checklist to examine the product • Document findings, results, and parking boards • Trace each requirement and document it on the requirements traceability matrix (RTM) **Facilitator should ask:** • Have any defects been identified? • What improvements are needed? • Who will make the improvements? • Have all the quality attributes been identified? • Is each requirement properly numbered and labeled? • Is each requirement allocated to the correct resource? • Have any constraints been identified? • What assumptions are being made? • Have any risks been identified? • Have any business rules been identified?	• Product to inspect • Inspection checklist and supporting tools • Questioning techniques • Discussion techniques
8. Summarize inspection results	Facilitator		• Provide summary of findings • Review next steps and associated timelines • Communicate when and where the results will be published **Facilitator should ask:** • Is there anything else to add? • Are there any changes or revisions to the documented results? • Do we have the commitment from participants to complete the follow-up actions?	• Post completed work on the wall for discussion • Repository guidelines • Communication plan

Figure 8-1—Deliverable Inspection Meeting Facilitator Agenda, continued

Topic	Presenter	Allotted Time	Facilitator Agenda	Facilitation Tools and Techniques
9. Review parking boards and next steps	Facilitator		• Review the parking boards. • Assign a due date and owner to each action item or issue for resolution. • Review next steps and associated timelines. This should include: • Issue resolution • Action items • Distribution of review results • Communicate when and where the review results will be published. • Inform the interviewee of the project repository location. **Facilitator should ask:** • Are there any questions? • Are there any corrections to the parking board items? • Does the team have your commitment to complete the assigned next steps?	• Parking board templates • Issues log • Action item log • Risk log • Constraints log • Parking lot • Project repository guidelines
10. Evaluate and close inspection	Facilitator and review team		• Review the goals and objectives. • Conduct an evaluation to validate whether the measures of success for the prototype session have been met. • Conduct a lessons learned discussion to identify ways to improve future reviews. • Thank participants for their time and contributions.	• Agenda with goals, objectives, and measures of success • Evaluation form or technique • Lessons learned template

Chapter 9

Closing Comments

Following a structured process to plan, facilitate, and follow up on business analysis meetings contributes to the quality of the requirements generated. As you develop your business analyst skills, focus on sharpening facilitation skills like listening, restating ideas for clarity and asking pointed questions, and the basics of meeting management. Hone your belief in the power of the team, demonstrate patience, and remain objective. In general, a good facilitator is energetic, respectful, and supportive of the team process. There is no substitute for experience. You will become better with each meeting. Take advantage of each experience to objectively evaluate your abilities to effectively use group process techniques, and grow with each experience.

To become a great facilitator, focus on the following development activities:

+ Enroll in facilitation classes.

+ Enroll in presentation and communication skills classes.

+ Consider becoming a professional certified facilitator.

+ Seek out a mentor who is a great facilitator.

+ Ask a great facilitator—or a good friend and colleague—to observe you in action and give you feedback.

+ Evaluate your effectiveness as a facilitator after each meeting.

If you are looking for a business analyst for your project, ensure that the applicant is a skilled facilitator. To assess a candidate's facilitation knowledge and skills, ask yourself questions such as:

+ Is the person a professionally certified facilitator?

+ Does the person have a good reputation as a facilitator?

+ How does the person design and plan for meetings?

+ Does the person have knowledge of business analysis meeting goals and content?

+ Does the person define meeting roles and responsibilities?

+ Does the person conduct premeeting research? How?

+ What facilitation tools does the person use?

+ How does the person bring teams to consensus?

+ What group dynamic techniques does the person use?

+ How does the person foster open and honest communication?

+ Is the person considered an expert in the business area undergoing change?

+ Does the customer think highly of the person?

+ Does the technical development team think highly of the person?

+ Is the person thought of as a leader? A consultant?

+ Is the person known for the ability to grasp both business and technical issues?

+ Can the person ask tough questions without seeming threatening?

Also of importance when selecting a business analyst is considering what a facilitator is not:

+ A subject matter expert on the issue at hand

+ An organizational strategist

+ A technical lead

+ A member of executive management

+ A participant who offers an opinion

Index

A

acknowledgment
(communication category), 34
affinity diagrams, 71–72
agendas
for business modeling
workshops, 116–126
for business process modeling
workshops, 116–126
conducting meetings using, 21–22
for deliverable inspection
meeting, 174–180
as management technique, 76
preparing, 14–18
for prototype review
meetings, 130–136
for requirements elicitation
interviews, 85–92
for requirements elicitation
workshops, 97–107
for requirements specification
review meetings, 154–166
for risk management
workshops, 139–148
tabling items on, 21
analysis. *See* group analysis skills
anonymous brainstorming, 69
artifacts, 16

B

bad faith, 35
behaviors, managing, 35, 76
binary searches, 69
brainstorming, 65–72
brainwriting, 69
break-out groups, 46–47
BSLC (business solution
life cycle), 61, 170
business modeling workshops
agenda for, 116–126
challenges, 111
meeting management, 111–113
participants in, 111
purpose and benefit, 110
business opportunities,
framing, 43–44
business problems, framing, 43
business process modeling workshops
agenda for, 116–126
challenges, 114
meeting management, 114–116
participants in, 114
purpose and benefits, 113–114
business solution life cycle
(BSLC), 61, 170

G

gap analysis, 50–51
ground rules, establishing, 19–21
group analysis skills
  break-out groups, 46–47
  facilitated discussions, 44–45
  flip charts, 47–48
  force field analysis, 52–53
  framing problems/
    opportunities, 43–44
  gap analysis, 50–51
  identifying interests, 42
  presentations, 45–46
  root cause analysis, 53–56
  separating content from
    process, 41–42
  storyboards, 48–50
  SWOT analysis, 51–52
group communication skills
  asking pointed questions, 58–60
  choosing words carefully, 57
  listening, summarizing,
    reframing, 57–58
group decision-making
  brainstorming in, 66–72
  consensus in, 63–65
  decision grids in, 74–75
  meeting ground rules for, 20
  multivoting in, 72–73
  nominal group technique in, 73–74
  options for, 63
  selecting process, 16
  surveys in, 65–66
group leadership, 60–62
group process models
  group decision-making, 62–75
  group leadership, 60–62
  keeping meetings on track, 75–77
guidance
  (communication category), 35

I

idea mapping, 69–70
informational meetings, 4
instruction
  (communication category), 35
interests, identifying, 42
interviews
  description, 4
  requirements elicitation
    via, 79, 81–92
Ishikawa diagram, 53–56

J

JAD (joint application design)
  workshop, 93
Jung, Carl, 32

K

knowledge café, 69

L

leadership
  facilitating style of, 42
  group, 60–62
  presentation style of, 42
  team, 61–63
lessons learned, collecting, 23

M

N

O

P